This book is dedicated to all those who helped create the world we live in, and all those who will help me continue the process.

A special thanks goes out to my wife, my sounding board, my proof reader, and my editor in chief: Keeza Anzini. I would also like to thank Heather, Jackie, Kathie and Michelle for their efforts to help make this book what it is.

May your
lessons Be Swift &
Memorable ENJOY!

CONTENTS:

How many psychologists does it take to change a light bulb?

Just one, but the light bulb has to *want* to change.

(Unknown)

CHANGE

Some would ask how do we change, or how do we get others to change? Questions about change bring up the old joke… So the question can quickly become, how do we make ourselves or others want to change? What makes us want change, or if we don't want change, what is it we do want? Do we want a new car, house, relationships, kids, or maybe just a big bag of cash? Finding our own answers to these and any other questions we can come up with, is a big part of "discovering who we are."

The question "How do I become a good person?" inspired me at a young age, to search from theology to philosophy to psychology back to philosophy, with an endless number of detours to find my truth. I read book after book, looking for the one that would tell me how to live my life. The search took roughly 19 years. In my 27th year on this earth, I felt I had finally found a truth large enough to make me worthy of my own respect. The respect I "lost" when I was told at eight years old, "You might not turn out to be a good person." In reality (like most of us), I had found many truths along my path. My ego told me none of the truth I had found was up to the standards required to reach the goal of "enlightenment."

I had found my first reversal; my first big truism, which gave me a glimpse at the bigger picture: Is it ever ok for someone to come into my life and tell me how to live, who to be and what to do? The answer was obviously no. So how can it be ok for me to tell someone *they* have to stay, bend or change because I love them, or just because "I said so?" In fact, if I love them, is it not my job to encourage them to do whatever *they* want, to *find their own* path? If the relationship is not satisfying *both* of us, honesty and fairness demand I let them and myself out of an uninspiring, stagnant situation.

In many ways, believing that I had finally reached true wisdom was a new beginning. I expected life to change with my newfound wisdom like flipping a switch. I realized all the truth I had found, and all the "wisdom" I had gained, was in preparation for another lesson. A famous musician once stated he practices his instrument 8 hours a day just to keep his skills at their current level. Enlightenment is not a destination; it is a path some choose to walk, if they are willing to do the work of practicing every day to stay on the path.

Some of the concepts in this book are not so small and require several sentences or paragraphs to be made clear. If things get a bit puzzling, read the sentence a few times, then continue to the end of the chapter. My wife and I placed these chapters in an order that works best for us. Since we are not all the same, some will need to read chapter six before chapter four will make sense. To others chapter five will be unnecessary and chapter seven will appear to be some kind of magic and so on.

Follow your passion, let your inspiration guide you, leap from the top of your personal mountain and learn to fly *again*. We must walk our path to learn who we are and what we can do. There are many circles in life, similar truths that can be found in many different places. Some truths are presented as "golden rules," or "big pictures," when they are more like a few illuminating pieces to a much larger puzzle. Other truths will fill gaps in these "golden rules" and "big pictures" we may have been unaware of. As we fill these gaps, it is easy to see we need to continue our search; as there are always more details to see and more to learn.

Our passions made us feel like we could fly when we were children; can we learn to fly again? What if our dreams and inspirations have been suppressed our whole lives? How do we find them again? How do we recognize the right path for ourselves? What makes us who we are? How do we find love, happiness and success?

This book is the result of my search for answers to these and many other questions. This collection started as an attempt to rewrite my reality. Sharing this knowledge has shown me many people can easily change the course of their lives and personal wellbeing, with just a little guidance. Taking a lesson from Leonardo Da Vinci, I have condensed many different sources of knowledge and wisdom, collected from many great teachers. I have studied many things and been an observer my entire life. This book is a list of my discoveries, distilled into what I hope you will find easily manageable and entertaining pieces.

Our time is now. The current pace of personal evolution in the world can occur much faster. We are standing on the precipice of mature global awareness. We are the ones who will either grow up and jump, or remain on the cusp of the next age of reason; frustrated in our self imposed stagnation. Come with me and find your *own* path. Allow yourself to see the way. Become stronger and more powerful than you have ever been.

~ IV ~

Open the door and take your first steps on a full path. Fill your world and I will see you there.

DESTINATION

From our first breath of air, the first time we ate or went to the bathroom, there was a desire for relief from some unexpected change in our situation. When we first move out into the world, we have to learn to breathe on our own. As we grow, we develop an idea of what comfort means to *us*. Depending on our abilities and the environment, we can become attracted to anything. Our hopes and dreams are born in our minds and we spend our lives moving toward these things, or we spend our lives "dealing with life."

Dealing with life is often moving *away* from what we *do not* want. As many of us have experienced, moving away from what we do not want often brings us full circle back to the same old rotten situation. Why do we become poorer when we say we do not want to be poor? Why do we end up in abusive relationships after swearing off abusive people? Life is like any other journey; we have to *know* where we are *going* in order to reach our destination.

To embark on a journey there must be a destination in mind, even if it is just a general direction like north. In order to begin a journey of the mind we must want something. What do you want? If you are like most of us, you want things like: wealth, fame, family, true friends, success, love etc. All of these things bring us something that starts very strong but fades with time.

When we win at a game of chance or skill, we feel confident. When we gain friendship, have a much anticipated child or find a better paying occupation, we feel successful, productive, happy etc. Without continued stimulation, the gains in self esteem we receive from these experiences fade over time. Can we imagine for a moment that it is not the car, the money or the success we want? Could it be the *self esteem* we get from attaining a goal, regardless of what that goal is?

There must be other ways to gain self esteem, besides collecting stuff: children, money, fame, sex, and control of others just to name a few. Self esteem comes from congruence with who we are, following our joy and passions to do positive, constructive things. Live our life for our self first.

- Giving *when* we can afford to

- Giving *where* we can afford to

- Giving *only* when we *want* to

Our thoughts can sometimes run away with us, leading us into depression, anxiety and other emotionally painful places. Many of us choose to dwell on why, what if, and other questions looking for the *cause*. When we *think* about the cause or inspiration for our emotional pain, it continues to *fuel* our *pain*. When dealing with emotional pain, the fastest way out is not to identify the cause, but to *focus* on the *outcome*. Focus on how we get out of the mental space of anxiety and depression. Ask, "What makes us feel better," and "what made us feel better the last time we experienced this?"

~Try This~

Ask the question *often*; what do I want? What is the destination, result or outcome I am looking for? How can I better prepare myself to answer the call when destiny rings? How can I make the *best* decisions *every* time I make a decision? The answers to these questions can only be found through observing ego.

OBSERVING EGO

We must observe ourselves every day in every way. Inside our head, say to our self, "Wow, look what I just thought, look what I just did, wow, this is an interesting feeling, an interesting desire," etc. Without our attention, the mind is at the whim of its environment. Ideas, instincts and emotions will continually fight for the leadership role of the body. Sometimes we will glut our hunger for food, sex, or other physical vices only to regret them later. How many times have we taken absolute control over our impulses, only to "fall off the wagon" again when our needs are not being met properly?

Observing ego is the beginning of the path to personal understanding. It takes a little practice but we must do whatever is needed to develop what is commonly referred to as: "observing ego." The more time spent watching the mind's thoughts, emotions and instincts, the easier observing ego will become. We will notice ourselves disagreeing with some of our actions, thoughts, words, attitudes, etc. only *after* we see ourselves do or think them.

~Try This~

Take note of the action, thought, word, etc. and when time permits, consider what motivated the undesirable actions, words, thoughts etc. After **taking note** a few times we will *notice* the actions, thoughts etc. *as they* occur. Eventually we notice we are heading in the direction of an undesirable action, behavior, attitude etc. and we change course **before we act**. We eventually notice we are *thinking* undesirable thoughts, feeling undesirable emotions and/or undesirable instinctual reactions, and edit the undesirables before they have a chance to influence our attitude or behavior.

When we catch ourselves doing something we don't approve of, make a new plan and decide what the perfect "us" would do or say. Next time we notice the same situation arising, use the new behavior. Affirm the new behavior, "I am so glad I do/use the new plan instead of the old way." See how our new plan works out and modify the plan again and again, each time an experience teaches us something new.

Observing ego is the way to edit our words, actions, and thoughts in real time, *before* we do them. Who of us has not said or done something we wished we could take back? What if we could *see* our internal processes and *know* when we were becoming irrational *before* we actually started acting or speaking irrationally?

We must practice observing ego constantly; the act of observing ourselves must be natural and normal. In the beginning, we will switch between observing ourselves critically, and acting on "auto pilot." When we indulge the ego by listening to all of its concerns, anxieties, predictions of the future, and regrets from the past, we are listening to the "internal dialogue." When we are listening to the internal dialogue, our actions are running on "auto pilot." We all have well trained minds that keep us entertained, concerned, driven, fearful, motivated, depressed, optimistic etc. The mind that keeps us occupied in this way is *distracting* us from life in the *present moment*.

When we are relaxed it is easy to watch our mind and body do their thing. As the internal dialogue starts to list all our plans, concerns etc. we become distracted and observing ego goes out the window. Later in the day, we will notice ourselves doing something and *remember* observing ego. As long as we remind ourselves daily, the instances of observation will become more and more common. Many new cars have headlights which turn on as soon as the car is started. After enough practice, we don't have to turn observing ego on. When we wake up in the morning, observing ego will be a normal part of our conscious mind.

Things get broken when our attention is divided. Observing ego allows us a few seconds of leeway.

For example:

- We *remember* we are holding a plate, while trying to scratch our arm, just before we spill the contents of our plate.
- We *remember* how angry discussing politics makes us, so we *change* the subject to avoid the issue until we can find a way through our anger.
- We know if we do not give ourselves a small snack before our commute home, we will binge eat when we get home.

Every morning, once we are fully awake, ask "where is my mind." Make mental notes or write down the answers to the following questions: what am I thinking, (logic) how do I feel (emotion) and how does my body feel? (instinct) When we first start paying close attention to the mind, there is a seemingly endless amount of verbalization about the future, the past, our pain, our pleasure, our discomfort etc. **Take note** of the feelings, emotions, sensations, inclinations, etc. When we pay close attention to our thoughts, the mind eventually grows silent or repeats itself.

After we do the "where is my mind" exercise the first few times, we will notice repetition and negativity we may have previously been unaware of. All our thoughts are *programming* from memories and experiences. The programs running through the mind are naturally occurring affirmations. Write down any thoughts from the past. Negativity and repetition are wonderful resources we can use to make up new positive replacement affirmations. Anyone with conscious thoughts in their head is already using affirmations; the trick is recruiting those affirmations to work *for* us and *attract* what we *want* into our lives, instead of attracting what we *don't want*.

The thoughts running through us are created by the influences we invite into our minds. The thoughts that stay *become* the internal dialogue, parent, coach, etc. As we get older, some of the things we say to ourselves become distorted, and no longer serve our best interests. Our job as enlightened beings is to continually edit and re-write the internal dialogue to match the person we want to be; to lead the life we wish to live. With just a few minutes a day spent rewriting our personal programs, things like happiness and fun become *decisions* and not a consequence of the outside world.

~Try This~

Changing thoughts into positive, personal, present tense statements can sometimes be a bit of a puzzle. Taking each requirement one at a time is the easiest way to go. What follows are some short examples of positive, personal, present tense affirmations, made from negative thoughts and the changes they underwent.

Examples:

The first thought we will work with is: "I am such an idiot." This thought is a negative thought which we will change to a positive affirmation. The negative part of this thought is the word "idiot," which is an antonym of words like pupil, savant, scholar, genius etc. To make this a positive affirmation, we simply choose an antonym for the negative or undesirable part of the thought. In this instance the statement could be: "I am such a genius."

The second thought we will work with is: "I will never finish this project." This thought is easy to change into its positive: "I will finish this project." However we live in the present; any future is a prediction *and* is out of our reach. We can only hope to influence the future with what we do *now*. We must change this thought from future tense to present tense. What can I do now to finish the project? All I can do is all I can do, so the affirmation becomes: "I do *all I can* to move this project toward completion."

Another thought we will work through is: "No one is going to like my… cake, song, fashion choices, etc." This thought needs a complete overhaul, to go from negative to positive, from future to present and from controlling others to personal. First we make it positive: we replace "no one" with "everyone" to get "Everyone is going to like my…" This is a great statement, but perhaps an emotional gamble and still in the future. We are all genetically wired to seek the acceptance of our peers, but the only acceptance we can guarantee is our own.

This thought seeks to interact with others, so how are we involved with others in our statement? We are sharing something of ours with our peers in the hopes of gaining some self esteem from *their* approval. So how do we enjoy sharing with everyone without seeking their approval? We base our happiness on the fact that we like who we are and what we have to give. How better to strengthen bonds with those who like the things we do, than to share with them what *we* like *because* we *like it*? The thought then becomes: "I am going to enjoy sharing my... with everyone."

We also need to make the statement present tense, as we can only enjoy the present moment. The final statement could look something like this, "I always enjoy: sharing my cake, singing my heart out, strutting my stuff, etc. with everyone."

It is important to come up with affirmations that work for *us*. When an undesirable thought creeps in, the affirmation must make sense *to us* in order to work. When the undesirable thought arises, the new thought should be its **antidote**, canceling out the power of the old thought. The walls of our reality are painted with our thoughts, emotions and instincts. Changing our thoughts will change our perception.

~Try This~

It is important to be able to make eye contact and hold it. Looking at anyone in the eyes can be a bit unsettling, but the ability to do so and relax is one of the keys to building and displaying confidence. So why not start with someone who will work with us: our reflection. Many of us do not like what we see in the mirror, so the first exercise is finding all the best parts of every expression. What about our smile makes us look happy; the warmth in our eyes, the curve of our lips? Make other expressions and discover or decide what is best about each; is it the way we flair our eyebrows, or how far our lower lip sticks out? With enough searching, we will begin to focus on our qualities instead of our faults. Before we know it, we will have *learned* to *like* what we see in the mirror.

When we look at ourselves we often start thinking to ourselves about our appearance. Listen to these thoughts as though you are a counselor, listening to a parent instructing their child, or a gym coach giving one of the students a pep talk. Is this a good parent or coach? What would the *perfect* parent or coach sound like?

We have all spent time pretending; from childhood games, to adult satire, sarcasm, practical joking etc. Now it is time to convince *our self* of some very important things. Look in the mirror and be the best actor or actress we have ever been; plead with our self, demand of our self and reason with our self. See which method or methods of convincing work best.

A few minutes a day is all that need be invested. Anything; ritual or behavior, done for 22 days in a row, becomes a habit. In the beginning I suggest picking some affirmations from the list. The list below has several examples that can be used as is, or as templates for customization.

- I rely on my own opinion.

- I am beautiful/handsome.

- I approve my decisions when I make them, no other approval is needed.

- I make friends easily.

- I make good decisions.

- In my life there are only lessons and successes. Either it works or I get to learn something new.

- I have all I need in this moment.

- I am relaxed in all situations.

- I speak my mind with tact.

- I enjoy being who I am.

- I have confidence in my abilities.

- I am worthy.

- I do courage as often as possible. (Confidence is increased with the act of being brave. Being brave is called courage. Courage is a verb.)

When practicing observing Ego, one pays attention to the internal dialogue; the words, thoughts, and images that run through one's head, unbidden, all day long. The reality we create and live in is a result of our internal dialogue. We paint all the things we observe with our judgments. The thoughts, words and images we see in our head can become far more real than reality. To gain the most benefit from our internal dialogue, we should write down the thoughts, beliefs and opinions we tell ourselves all day and turn them into affirmations; positive present tense statements. Spend a few minutes every day writing the improved affirmations once and then reading them into the mirror.

During the day ask, "What am I thinking and doing?" Compare what we are thinking and doing with what we *want* to be thinking and doing. Be realistic, no ruling the world, dodging bullets, stopping trains, or jumping over buildings.

"Where are you Dan?" *"Here."* "What time is it?" *"Now."* "What are you?" *"This moment."* ~Peaceful Warrior 2006

MEMES

The concept of the meme (Richard Dawkins, "The Selfish Gene") is useful for maintaining the clarity of one's mind. Many thoughts and ideas are very persistent and greedy for the real-estate between our ears. Without an understanding of memes, we are allowing anything from our environment to *invade* our minds. Over time, invasive and insistent thoughts can and *do* push our beliefs in directions we may not want them to go.

Our minds are fertile soil for thoughts, images, emotions, etc. There are advertisements, songs, jokes, experiences and other thoughts that we often cannot seem to remove from our conscious mind, once they "take root." Many of us have experienced a tune from a commercial that the mind replayed over and over, long after the commercial was finished. Many of us have heard a joke that was in poor taste but could not wait to repeat the joke, poor taste or not. The main job of our mind is to record all kinds of information. Sometimes the information we record can be negative, damaging, or just plain unsavory.

I have observed myself and others say things like "oh my god that's terrible," only to take three steps and share the "terrible" information with a new person. Our minds can be used the same way a virus uses a healthy cell. The meme: an idea, belief, image, melody etc. will be recorded the same way a virus uses the resources of a healthy cell to make a copy of the virus. The meme will be *insistent* in the fore front of our mind; we will repeat it with little or no effort to anyone who will listen. By repeating the meme, we have just infected another person with a copy of the meme, the same method a virus uses to spread itself.

The memes do not care about our well being. The only thing a meme cares about is making copies of itself. Once we start listening to our thoughts as though they could be bad for our health and happiness, we become aware of many negative or detrimental behaviors, beliefs, phrases, feelings etc. All these beliefs, phrases, behaviors, feelings and thoughts are considered memes. What we say and do all day affirms our beliefs, outlook on life and reality in general. Weather thoughts are good or bad, they can be considered naturally occurring affirmations. Write down or **take note** of the memes in our mind. Decide if the memes are helping us or hurting us. Come up with replacements for any memes that fall short of things a *perfect* coach, parent, friend and/or guardian would say.

"There are people who lift you up, and people who drag you down, you have to decide who your friends are for yourself." I have heard the previous phrase from many different sources, in many different ways, while the message stayed the same. We ourselves are our last line of defense, not mom or dad, not our spouse or our best friend. We *ourselves* are the only ones we can count on to be with us everywhere we go. We are the *only* ones who have *our* unique perspective *constantly*. We must be on guard to protect our self from memes that seek to drag us down. The down dragging memes range from vices to antisocial behavior and beyond. Anything that is in our mind, but not serving our best interests, is a meme that needs to be uprooted or rewritten.

Verbal memes can be rewritten positively and used to counteract the negative memes when they arise. Simply read the positively phrased meme when the negative meme tries to assert itself. For quicker reprogramming, read the positive memes in the mirror at least once a day. Take advantage of the opportunity to improve any acting skills while reading the replacement memes. Say the new memes with feeling and make them real. The more often and convincingly we hear our new memes, the faster they will replace the old memes.

See also: Reflection and Observing Ego.

~Try This~

Verbal Thought test: Imagine a table with a few chairs, like a board room or meeting table. Now imagine the voices of opinion, experience, knowledge, peers etc. (verbal memes) that we hear inside our heads, are going to take physical form (tall or short, thick or thin, dark or light, etc.) The memes will now open the door to the imaginary meeting room, walk into the room and take a seat at the table.

Imagine how the verbal memes would dress according to their attitude, how they would walk according to their attitude. Imagine how the verbal memes would look as they said the things they said, according to their attitude. Does this person look or behave like a friend? Do they look or behave like someone you would let your children play with? Do you want to have them over for a barbecue? If the answer to any of these questions is no, perhaps the verbal meme should be rephrased to **be** more positive, encouraging, respectful and mature.

Behavior test: Testing a behavior is about respecting the behavior. Can we respect the behavior from any point of view? Do we like it when others behave in that way? Do we think the behavior is cool for everyone involved? If any parts of the behavior are unacceptable, would we be happy playing the part that was unacceptable? If the answer to any of these questions is no, perhaps the behavior could use some modification.

Belief test: To test a belief simply ask how many times it happens a day. A fear of being mugged is very real in many places in the world. Some places however, do not have many muggings at all. When asking this question of a belief, one can find out just how real a belief is. Ask friends and neighbors about your beliefs; find out if they have experienced any of these feared situations. The belief test is good for fears like: alien abduction, robbery, rudeness from strangers, poisoned food etc. It is important to be careful of any threat, but it is *also* important not to spend our every waking moment in fear or apprehension of life.

Infection by depressing or sad memes brings a whole new meaning to the term "mental illness." Many memes have evolved to work together. Both Jealousy and suspicion can be problematic for a relationship but together, they can and *do* cause serious issues. Many negative memes are easily passed from one person to another. When one person in a relationship is feeling taken advantage of, left out, or unloved, the mention of possible infidelity can ignite a fuse to the bomb that will destroy the relationship.

Often times it is a few simple destructive ideas that create an avalanche of angry people. When people are emotionally charged, they often seek to recruit others to their cause, in other words: to infect others with their emotions. We are all social creatures and strong emotions are easily spread. The angry mob is created by the spread of angry memes. One person tells another about their emotionally charged experience, idea, or understanding (meme or memes) and *together*, they tell more people. Eventually a group of angry people, infected with the same memes, are all charged up together. The idea that made the mob angry *does not care* about the safety of the people in the mob; it *only cares* about spreading itself.

We must keep a close watch on our emotions or we too will become infected with other people's attitudes. The emotional mind does not understand time, but it does understand experience. What made us angry once can certainly make us angry again. We do not make our best decisions with our emotions, instincts or thoughts alone. Complex, long-term decisions are best made by the *entire* mind. When instinct is satisfied, emotions are clam, and thought is willing to learn and try something new, we are operating at our best.

An awareness of our processes is the best virus protection for the supercomputer called the mind. Without our awareness to protect us, our minds are like a computer on the internet downloading and installing every piece of software we can find. Anyone who owns a computer knows one good virus will wipe out a computer. How many detrimental memes do we want to grow inside of us and spread to our friends and loved ones? It is amazing our minds continue to function with so many contradicting and self destructive programs, all running at the same time. Next time we talk to someone who is emotionally charged or full of ideas, *watch* our own processes. Ask our self "how are their emotions and ideas affecting me?" "Are my emotions or thoughts changing?" "Are new ideas or emotions *taking root* in *my* mind?" "Do I want to be, *like them*?"

"To eliminate the weeds, one must pull out their roots. To work for acceptance means to uproot all traces of one's cultural heritage and former identity." ~Wang. 1991, Zhancao zhugen

SELF HYPNOSIS

Hypnosis is a method of clearing up, or calming the *entire* mind. Hypnosis is what we experience during activities like: meditation, prayer, exercise, watching a great movie, and even cuddling with our loved ones. We can discover many other ways to experience the clarity sought through hypnosis. Hypnosis teaches us to calm our mind and create mental paths to our goals in life, and in personal growth. Hypnosis is a dry run or rehearsal for our mind to make clear our wants, needs and desires. Hypnosis uses the law of attraction through words, visualizations, textures, tastes and smells to help us navigate our own internal processes and external experiences.

~Try This~

Simple hypnotic trance: Find a comfortable spot away from disturbances. Use pillows, earmuffs, even a sleeping mask if necessary to make the outside world recede. We want to create a situation where as much of our attention can be focused inward as possible.

There are many visualizations which can be used to help further relax one's body and clear one's mind. Some of us have very busy minds and will need images with lots of stimulation for added relaxation and clarity. Ocean waves are an example of a visualization with a good deal of stimulation. Some may have an easier time clearing their mind of random thought and can use simpler visualizations, like the "basement" example that follows.

Ocean waves: Imagine sitting on a beach in a comfortable spot, a folding chair, sand hill, and your significant other's lap. *See and hear* the waves gently rising, cresting and crashing on the shore. *See* the sunlight glittering on the surface of the water and lighting up the tiny droplets of ocean spray from the crashing waves. *Smell* the salt in the air from the oceans spray. *Smell* your favorite sun block/tan lotion on your skin. *Feel* the warmth of the sun on your skin, your cloths, your hat etc. Feel the warm air or cool breeze that is caressing your skin, keeping you at a perfectly comfortable temperature. Find as many details in the visualization as possible for each of the senses... "And with the crashing of each wave on the beach, I feel my mind and body relaxing deeper and deeper..."

Basement of the mind: "As we open the door to relaxation by closing our eyes, we see a doorway of the mind leading down a staircase, spiraling into the basement of the subconscious. As we place our foot on the first step, we begin to feel more relaxed and find it easier to breath. With another step, we find our thoughts receding and our body growing even more relaxed, more comfortable. With each step, our body becomes even more relaxed and our mind becomes quieter," and so on.

Any visualization that has a repetitive element, like stairs and waves, can be useful for inducing a trance. Here are some examples of visualizations I have used to induce trance:

- Wind blowing through tree leaves
- Water dropping from a stalagmite into a pool, in an underground cave filled with crystals

- Water trickling over rocks in a stream
- The crackle of a camp fire burning

Pick something you like, something relaxing, and create a visualization that works best for you. For an especially relaxing trance, record yourself reciting your chosen visualization. Walk yourself through an entire session on the recording. Speak in soothing, rhythmic tones. Repeat each part of the visualization at least three times, alternating the statements including the words: "body, muscles, become more relaxed, mind becomes clearer."

Example of fire used in visualization: "You find yourself sitting in a comfortable chair, next to a fire and feel the heat of the burning wood warming your face and skin. The hiss and crackle of the fire is unpredictable, so soothing you find yourself closing your eyes in relaxation. Each crack of the burning wood snaps away a thought about work, traffic, or drama trying to cloud your mind. The warmth of the fire is like a blanket muffling all the thoughts in your head. The fire's blanket of warmth is making the thoughts fade away. The thoughts are getting lost in the background. Listening to the hiss of the fire is like listening to the breath of a sleeping loved one. You sit comfortably with the rhythmic breathing in the near silence. The warmth of the fire makes your muscles relax as you sink into the comfortable chair, relaxing even deeper. The hiss and crackle of the fire is like an ancient language of tranquility, whispering clarity into your mind. As you listen to the sounds of the fire, your mind becomes expectant for the next crack, pop and hiss of the flames. The language of the fire seems to be caressing and calling to the older parts of your awareness. As you relax, the heat and sound of the fire, caresses and sooths your body and mind with its gifts of even more relaxation and clarity. The heat and sounds of the fire are calling you deeper into this place of comfort and clarity."

For the next part of the process, we choose the things we wish to: *notice* with our awareness, *hear* in our thoughts and *feel* in our beliefs. Write down or record some affirmations and/or positive things we would like to have more awareness of in life. Record the positive statements to have them ready for trance.

When I was a young man and was stuck in my anger, I used hypnosis to visualize people holding hands, kissing, laughing etc. I believed everyone was angry, upset, or lying. I would use my voice recorder to record the imagery I wanted for my trance. I would then record statements like: "you notice people having fun all around you, you notice lovers holding hands and kissing, you notice groups of friends walking, talking together and laughter fills the air all around you. You are calm and confident interacting with strangers. People enjoy listening to you. People enjoy talking to you." This work with self hypnosis allowed me to see things I was previously unable to see.

Breathe: Every time I induce trance in myself, I first take a deep, cleansing breath and close my eyes as I exhale. Take full, deep breaths and make sure to *exhale completely*. Breathing is a large part of relaxation. Find a comfortable pace for your breathing and maintain it throughout your trance. Choose or create a visualization, to relax the body and clear the mind. If we find our mind still talking about something other than the visualization, we must increase the number of things going on in the visualization to effectively distract the mind. Sometimes just saying the visualization more rapidly, with more repetition, can be enough to distract and/or clear the mind. Once we are firmly in our trance, play the recorded positive statements. Pay attention to our visualization and let the recorded statements play in the background. Maintain the visualization as long as possible, while playing the positive statements. The effectiveness of this exercise increases the more it is used so repeat as often as possible.

Once the process of self hypnosis has been done a few times, a simple deep breath and a slow exhale become a trigger to calm the body and mind. We sometimes find ourselves in stressful situations and wish there was a way to become suddenly calm. Hypnosis teaches our body to respond to our breathing with calmness and clarity.

When I wish to induce trance on the fly, I take a deep cleansing breath and close my eyes as I exhale. After one more breathe, I open my eyes refreshed and focused; as though I had just gone through an *entire* hypnotic session. During the brief moment my eyes are closed, I will often make a quick, simple motivational statement. Example: "I'm the man, we've got this, here we go, one more time, light as a feather, easy now, etc." To command the strongest response from our body, we should induce trance in the same way, making a ritual of it. Over time, recreating the clarity and relaxation found in trance will become easier and easier.

~Try This~

Hypnosis on the fly: When I arrive for an important meeting, whether it is business or pleasure, I will take one extra moment in my car to take a deep, cleansing breath to ready myself for the meeting ahead. In moments of stress, like traffic issues or confrontations, simply taking the cleansing breath will do wonders for our ability to steer the situation toward its best outcome.

When a situation does not go the way we want it to, induce trance and *visualize* the situation as we would have liked it to turn out. Take for example someone going to job interviews all day and so far all the people have been unkind and disinterested. Before the next interview, take a moment and visualize going into a business where people are positive and happy to meet you. The person conducting the interview is amazed at your resume. The interviewer is eagerly asking you questions, becoming more and more excited, until they offer you the job right on the spot.

People can read our motivation on our faces. If we are tired and disinterested, people will see it. Often times, motivation and positivity make people more likely to help us and give us a job, loan, house, car etc. Recharging our motivation with a moment of self hypnosis, may be the final piece that helps us get things done. Hypnosis also takes advantage of the law of attraction, which works by visualizing situations and things we want to attract into our life. Finally, this exercise helps us develop a better relationship with our selves, which over time increases our ability to *call up* some clarity and calm whenever we need it.

~Try This~

Inducing states: Pick a feeling, emotion or attitude we wish to experience: confidence, arousal, relaxation, alertness, drowsiness, etc. Picture a person we have seen in the desired state, like James Bond for confidence or a hibernating bear for drowsiness. *Remember* a time when we *experienced* the state. Think of all the things our body feels and does in that state.

To induce drowsiness, one might imagine heavy muscles, slow movements and droopy eyes. To be alert, pick one's head up, let one's eyes devour the surroundings, interested in every detail of everything. Quicken one's breathing, straighten posture, etc. Imagine a person in the state we want to experience, is that person sitting, standing or laying down? Make our body congruent with the desired state. Concentrate on *feeling* the things related to the desired state.

The first state I decided to memorize was happiness and I found it in a smile. I remember a time when I was very happy. Imagine an image of our self smiling sincerely and uncontrollably. Many of us will find it difficult *not* to feel some of the joy in the memory of happiness. Many of us will also find it difficult *not* to smile when imagining ourselves smiling. With state induction, the sincere smile is *always available* to help *make us feel good.*

State memorization: Once you have successfully induced a state, try to locate in your body, where you *feel* the state. For example, my happiness feels like it starts in my solar plexus. Give the feeling a color; my happiness color is like a camp fire, flickering red, orange and yellow. Give the feeling a texture; my happiness texture is like warm towels on my skin, fresh out of the dryer or off the cloths line on a sunny day. For a stronger connection, do this exercise while in trance.

Any time we are not feeling absolutely happy, focus on the color, texture, feeling and images we have associated with our happiness. With practice, memorizing the feelings of happiness and wellbeing will allow us to directly encourage our mind to release chemicals which make us feel better. The mind is like a muscle, the more we practice this and other mental exercise, the stronger the results will be.

State wrapping: Sometimes we are experiencing states that are unpleasant. Pick an undesirable state and then find a way to *wrap it* in another, less unpleasant state.

Example: Anger at other cars and/or drivers in traffic. **First wrap -** curiosity: be curious and think about how many times a day one is angry in traffic. **Second wrap** – amusement: Isn't it funny, how easily others can push our buttons by the way they drive. **Third wrap** – Humor: imagine a score card like those used in golf, where a lower score is better. Keep score by keeping track of how many times we get angry in a day. Also like golf, you can watch your score improve over particular courses: driving to and from work, a business meeting with Jim, getting the kids to school, dinner with relatives, etc.

Create an emotional path *away* from vice-like emotional indulgences like anxiety, insomnia, anger, binge eating, smoking drinking, you get the idea. Find something that relates easily to the unhelpful feeling or behavior. Imagine a time when we were experiencing an unhelpful feeling or behavior, then imagine shifting this behavior or feeling into a *different* feeling or behavior. With enough practice, when the emotion arises, we will notice how easy it is to shift to the next, less stressful, layer of emotion and behavior.

Internal communication: Some urges and desires do not respond well to words. Often times *telling* ourselves we are on a diet, or lactose intolerant, does not take away the *desire* for cake or ice cream. Emotional and physical memory are useful tools for communicating to the subconscious; when an over indulgence in desires like candy, drugs, or sex, may lead to discomfort, disease and sometimes even death.

Most people have experienced indigestion from rich or spicy foods, or a stomach ache from too much sugar. When the desire to overindulge in something arises, think about the *feeling* of discomfort from our last over indulgence in candy, drugs, sex or whatever. After *remembering* the feeling of discomfort from our last overindulgence, we may find the desires fading.

The other half of this method is to offer the subconscious a suitable replacement. We must always provide solutions when we are faced with restrictions, like natural sugar in a piece of fruit instead of the sugar in a piece of cake. When all we do is restrict and limit ourselves, our subconscious will naturally seek an opportunity to rebel. Losing our temper and binge eating are two common forms of subconscious rebellion. More information regarding subconscious rebellion can be found in "Raising The Animal."

Language patterns: How we speak to ourselves and others, speaks volumes about *our* perspective on life. Many words have connections to emotions, some do not. Words like: bacon, fire, candy, wind-chill etc. all have direct connections to our emotions and instincts. Words like: don't, can, have, is, etc. are not as strongly connected to our emotions and instincts. The subconscious does not understand semantics. Examine the following sentences:

I am happy. I am not happy. I am sad. I am not sad.

The feelings related to these statements are not the same as the logical intent of the words. When we speak the word "happy," we have emotional connections to this word; experiences, feelings, and images we have labeled "happy." The first two sentences in the example are *more* positive than the last two. When we speak the word "sad," we have emotional connections to this word; experiences, feelings and images we have labeled "sad."

The words *surrounding* the emotionally charged words often do not influence our internal state. The subconscious hears these words as if they are a foreign language. The subconscious does not know the meanings behind the words; it only understands the emotion, tone and the *way* the words are said. Close attention must be paid to the state related words we use in our daily verbalizations, aloud or to ourselves. When we *take note* of our language patterns, we can insert more positive state related words. This will teach the subconscious to *believe* we are indeed looking for happiness in our lives.

~Try This~

Useful visualizations: Think of sometime or somewhere you are *completely* comfortable being yourself. Imagine instances or situations where you can be authentically yourself, say whatever you want to say and know that you will be accepted, even if you are not understood. When the image of this comfortable place is clear in your mind, allow yourself to be *in* it, *experiencing* it, *living* it. Let the image *become* reality and then memorize the state. Use the memory of the comfortable state when walking on stage to deliver a speech, when interviewing for a job, or meeting a friend in a new bar or restaurant. I am always completely comfortable in my living room. When going to a place where I am not comfortable, I just imagine I am walking into my new living room.

Remember or imagine a person you can always be comfortable and relaxed around, then memorize the state. Use this state when meeting new people, asking strangers for directions, advice about local dining options, meeting your significant others parents for the first time, etc. My younger brother is one of the people I feel completely comfortable and relaxed around. Whenever I meet someone new I imagine what I would say to my brother in such a situation.

Imagine a person behaving in a way you have only seen or heard about but admire. Focus on the emotions that reside in a person *doing* the things you admire. What is the admirable person thinking, is their mind clear of thought, are they reciting a mantra, what is their motivation? Once you have the feelings and motivations figured out, memorize the state. Use this state to feel strong when you are in a trying situation, like being accused unfairly, finishing a particularly difficult paper, when debating a disagreement, etc. When I was working on the larger college projects, I would sometimes feel like I was not making enough progress and that I was not going to make my deadline. I would ask myself, "What would have happened if Einstein had given up in school?" "What would have happened if Benjamin Franklin had given up after the first 100 light bulb filaments did not work?" "What if the Wright brothers had given up after their first crash?" Suddenly the size of my project is almost laughable; I accept that all paths lead forward, check in with the subconscious to make sure everything is ok, and then it's back to work with new energy and tenacity borrowed from my heroes and idols.

Find other useful states and memorize them. The mind has amazing power to help the body. We can use this power to improve our life and our satisfaction with life.

"You use hypnosis not as a cure but as a means of establishing a favorable climate in which to learn." ~Milton H. Erickson, MD

TWO BOXES

From the time we first pop into the world, we are expected to learn what to do and what not to do. In order to survive we must make a list of behaviors, both acceptable and unacceptable. We are told how to be and how not to be, by authority figures, our environment and peers throughout our life. Some examples of early behaviors include learning to walk, talk, and handle our bodily functions.

Once we learned to walk and talk, many of us left these basic skills on what some refer to as "auto pilot." Auto pilot continues to perform old tasks exactly as we had originally learned to do them. We have all experienced distraction while performing a mundane task, only to look down and see our task was done while we were distracted. Often the tasks done while distracted, will not be our best work.

We have all been encouraged to do our best at one point or another. Doing our best on any task requires clarity, or the lack of distraction. We quickly chose role models for everything we wanted to learn. Some of us took an active interest in adding to the list of things we wanted to do/be and things we did not.

An easy way to visualize this "trait collection," is to imagine two puzzle boxes; an "I am" puzzle box, and an "I am not" puzzle box. Everyone in the world is the result of all the decisions they have ever made. We are all like a jigsaw puzzle with thousands, even millions, of pieces. When we see a trait/decision we like, or don't like, we take that piece and put it in one of our boxes.

We continue to collect pieces of "what I would like to be" and "what I would not like to be," till we reach puberty. Once we reach puberty, new chemicals released into our brains motivate us to become adults and help define who we are for ourselves. At this point, we open the two boxes, get out the mental scissors and glue, and start creating the picture that is to be our personality. Completing our puzzle will make us *our own* biggest influence. The first big chemical push for a completed puzzle comes at puberty.

We take ideals, morals and behaviors from vastly different people; so there will be contradictions that must be worked out. The puzzle must be made to fit together in such a way that each piece *complements* all the others. We must create an image we can understand for us to be a functional person. The more smoothly our puzzle fits together, the more confident we are in the personality we have created.

Once we are engaged in the process of assembling the collage that is to be who we are and who we are not, any new information thrown into the mix can interrupt this delicate process. We are creating a balanced image with the pieces we have collected. New pieces thrown on top of our collage will only confuse the image we have created thus far.

Some think teenagers are suddenly rebellious at puberty, when in fact they are simply building their adult self. Puberty is a time to reason with adolescents, as they are trying to solidify the foundation of who they will and won't be as adults. No longer does the budding adult do what he or she is told without question. Those who have enjoyed influence over these budding adults in the past may resent the sudden loss of command. To the guardian or parent who does not recognize this change, it suddenly appears that their little angel has become a "problem child."

The first tool we learn to use to communicate is emotion; in the form of crying, cooing, gurgling etc. Children grow up using emotional communication to influence those around them. Emotional communication requires energy: crying, screaming, flailing etc. As we learn to talk, we attempt to reason with those around us. Reason and logic do not require the same amount of energy as emotional communication.

As we mature, our logic and reason begin to negotiate without having to resort to an emotional rollercoaster to meet our needs. The more negotiation and debate a child engages in, the more they will begin to use reason and logic to get what they want. Without reason, a child has to resort to emotional blackmail (tantrums, back talk, deceit, etc.) to meet his or her needs. Every time a child is ignored, put off, given *no reason,* i.e. "because I said so," the child is being *taught reason does not work*. A situation that *does not allow* a child to *reason* and *negotiate,* **teaches** them they **must** use emotional blackmail to meet their needs. When reason does not work, a child does what he or she has to and resorts to older forms of communication like crying, screaming, flailing etc. Solely relying on emotional blackmail to negotiate can (and far too often does) create immature "adults" who *can only negotiate using emotion*. These pseudo adults often rely on behavior such as eye rolling, yelling, silence, anger, etc. instead of using logic and reason to get what they want.

If we use our emotions too often to negotiate, our emotions can end up *using us*. Confrontations become scripted by previous emotionally charged interactions. We can get stuck replaying scripted arguments or confrontations we have pre-written using emotionally charged events from our past. Every negotiation has opportunity for change and growth, but when all confrontations are seen as the same, no one learns, no one changes, and no one grows.

Many young adults going through this process recognize they are not being treated with respect from those who say things like: "I am only thinking of what is best for you." While these may be honest statements, they lay bare their own ignorance of the fact that their child is an *individual*, with his or her *own* dreams. How can some parents, guardians, or anyone truly believe they can dictate happiness to their children, when so many do not understand, let alone maintain, their own happiness?

Individuation "a.k.a. teen rebellion," is the last chance to help children sharpen their negotiating skills. Designing our adult selves during puberty is a genetic push for individuality. This push guaranties conflict with any oppressing, "because I said so," or "do as your told," influences.

Convince children through discussion and help their minds *learn* to make their *own* decisions, *rely* on their *own* judgment and confidently *choose* their *own* path. This is an opportunity for children to find out how to bargain, argue and debate, in a safe environment with people who should be happy to teach them to be the best negotiators they can be.

RE-BEGINNING

There comes a time in everyone's life when we decide we are not happy with what is going on. Some of us are lucky enough to get really upset and break something valuable as a permanent reminder of our frustration. Looking down at the broken pieces of a vase, T.V., relationship, or window, we decide we would do anything to be rid of this anger, rid of the drama, the stress, the anxiety, and all the broken stuff.

Unfortunately most of us then go and do something to help us forget our troubles. If we manage to succeed at forgetting, we find ourselves back at the beginning of the first paragraph. To break the circle of self destruction through distraction, we must not *allow* ourselves to *become* distracted. Instead of watching our internal processes as a participant, we must watch them as a spectator and a critic.

~Try This~

Here are some examples of questions we can ask ourselves to become more aware of our internal processes.

- What was happening in my mind just before I had a meltdown or confident decision?

- What was my mood: lonely, aroused, sad, happy, frustrated, relaxed, etc. just before the situation went sideways or perfectly?

- How was my body feeling: tired, hungry, threatened, comfortable, etc. when I made a good or bad: move, decision, statement etc.?

Awareness of our internal processes is the key to understanding who we have become and how to make the changes we want.

Our minds are pre-wired with underlying needs, wants and desires like: food, mating opportunities, companionship, safety, etc. We are told, when we are very young, what is possible and what is impossible, or just "against the rules." Our underlying needs, wants etc. may be unchangeable, but that is not what we are taught. Our parents and/or guardians play a large role in determining what makes us angry, happy, sad, comfortable, scared, desirable, left out, nervous, and so on.

We all re-evaluate our decisions about our likes and dislikes as we grow and mature. The process of reevaluation can be interrupted and sometimes stopped by an oppressive environment. An oppressive environment does not give us the freedom to make our own mistakes and learn our own lessons. Many of us, who are oppressed on a regular basis, stop the process of reevaluation at one age or another. With enough oppression, we *learn* it is *easier* to *allow* our parents, guardians and peers to permanently plant *their* decisions in *our* subconscious, never to be modified again. In other words, we give up our freedom to make our own decisions and choose how to live our own life. Most of us can make a better decision today than we could earlier in life. The emotional energy wrapped up in the decisions of the past still influence us today.

Most of us have heard the phrase; "Fool me once shame on you, fool me twice shame on me." The experience of betrayal, from a little white lie, to complete abandonment, can turn in to any number of emotional decisions like: suspicion, fear, anger, depression etc. No one wants to be fooled again, so when we recognize a situation is heading in a familiar direction, the emotion stored in the memory of betrayal *influences* and sometimes *dictates* our reaction. (See definitions "Reaction.")

Nervous people can often look the same as people who are trying to hide their dishonesty. When interviewing a perspective worker or being asked for a large favor, we will often see signs of nervousness. Even when we read the signals wrong, *emotional memory **does not care***, it merely influences our decisions based on the recognized signals. Those who are used to being mislead can easily confuse the signs of nervousness with the signs of dishonesty.

Abusive parents who profess their love can teach us to desire abuse as a part of "love." Bad relationships plague those whose definition of love includes some type of abuse. There are many good relationships and opportunities we miss out on because we are still making the *same* decisions we made previously. We continue choosing to have relationships with the same type of people.

When all we receive is criticism on our efforts to achieve, strive and create, we may grow up *believing* nothing we do is ever quite good enough. Dissatisfaction and a sense of inability to achieve something worth praise, follow those who see themselves as not quite good enough. We can achieve and create prosperity, beauty and happiness where ever we go. The tragedy is, when we do not recognize the value we are capable of creating, we cannot add our value to the world.

As we experience life, we connect our experiences with other similar experiences from our past. Any emotional content in similar *past* experience is **added** to our *present* experience. We get a dose of happy, or angry, or whatever, ***on top*** *of what we are already feeling.* The extra emotion from our past can quickly escalate the present emotion unrealistically; suddenly we are screaming and yelling about the cap being left off the toothpaste. Unrealistic escalations of emotion are one of the reasons we have arguments about the most foolish subjects. The present moment is "the straw that broke the camel's back," and all the past emotional content we carry with us **in** our experiences, is often one straw shy of a back breaking load.

Anyone who wants to stay in the sad, depressing, angry world of anxiety they have created, stop reading now! Otherwise, let's remove the emotional pressure from negative events in our past. Let us make our decisions as the person we are ***today***, with all of our resources and experiences; instead of continuing to live under the self imposed oppression of our emotionally charged past. As long as we deny or put up with this emotional influence from our past, we will continue to have the same type of experiences. We will continue to be attracted to the ones who hurt us and repel the ones who will actively help us grow and mature as human beings.

The first method I learned to remove emotional energy from memory is called recapitulation. Recapitulation is the reclaiming of emotional energy, or erasing the past. (Carlos Castaneda, *The Eagles Gift,* 1982) Recapitulating the past allows us to once again make fresh decisions as to how we will act in the face of new experience. Instead of being a slave to our past, we are free to decide if we want to get emotional and if so, how much emotion we want. There are several ways to accomplish this emotional remodel of our memories. A procedure called EMDR is a tool of psychotherapists that employs methods similar to recapitulation to accomplish a similar goal. (*Eye Movement Desensitization and Reprocessing*, Shapiro, F. 1989)

~Try This~

Recapitulation: Find a relaxing place where we will not be disturbed. Find a comfortable position. Breathe in and out slowly; try to count at least three or four seconds for the inhale and three to four seconds for the exhale. Turn our head from left to right as far as possible with comfort. Start with our head to one side, breath in slowly as we turn our head all the way to the other side. Once we reach the other side, breathe out and turn our head all the way back to the beginning side. This exercise is supposed to be relaxing; take it slow and get comfortable with the breathing and the movement. For extra comfort and positive sensation, try recapitulation in the shower or a hot bath.

Synchronize the breathing and the movement before moving on. If we cannot comfortably turn our head, we can look left and right (eyes open or closed) we can rotate our torso, rock back and forth, rub our hands up and then down our thighs. The point is to have a physical sensation that can be *synchronized* with the breathing. In order to *teach* the mind emotions in memories are *no present threat*, we must attach some calming, relaxing sensations and feelings to the memory.

The goal is to teach the mind that our experiences are just that: *past* events stored as memory with emotional content. We will be reviewing emotionally charged moments in our experiences. The more attention we have to pay to the present, the less attention and therefore power the memory receives. A memory that can usually make us cry will hopefully only bring a few tears while using this method.

Pick a past event that is unpleasant to think about. Start small; recapitulation frees our emotional energy. The "larger" the event, the more stored emotional energy we will have to deal with. To look at our experience objectively and use it to learn, grow and adapt, our experiences must *lose* their ability to push our emotional buttons. Recapitulation gives us power over our memories and experiences. Recapitulation allows us the opportunity to face our fears and grow some confidence in our strength to weather the storms of experience.

Start as early in the memory of the event as possible. Watch the event from beginning to end, remembering all the while to *breath* in and out *and move*. Pick one event or memory and watch it more than once. Notice the second or third time through, the memory has less emotional power. One day later, the same memory may have become emotionally boring. Some memories are less pleasant than others, so take small bites.

~Try This~

Use visualization to create emotional distance between us and particularly powerful memories. Watch the event in black and white; pretend we are in a theater watching the event in black and white. At any moment, we can get up and walk out of the theater, leaving the painful memory behind. The event will be easier to watch with each recapitulation of it. Recapitulation desensitizes us to our memories so we can remember them without *re-experiencing* unpleasant emotions.

~Try This~

Tell our self we are going to do some recapitulating. Take a full breath in, hold it for a fraction of a second and let it out. Notice how much more solid the idea of doing some recapitulating felt after the deep breath. Imagine a vice we would be happy to be rid of like smoking or over eating. Take a normal breath and make sure to breathe out as much as possible. Notice how the idea of the vice loses some of its power or fades in importance. During recapitulation the breathing is used similarly. Breathing in *completely* helps us to accept what is ours, and breathing out *completely* helps us release what we no longer need. With each inhale, we reclaim **our** energy stored in the memory; with each exhale, we release the energy of **others** also stored in the memory.

Recapitulation can bring up forgotten memories. Some of the new memories will simply be a memory with information. Other memories will have emotional content as well. Any emotional content we no longer wish to experience can be recapitulated. Every day emotionally charged events and interactions can be recapitulated, to help find issues we have hidden in our past. People who push our emotional buttons are actually doing us a favor. They help us by pointing out the kinds of things that activate our emotions.

Every time we become activated, it is a sign there is emotional energy we can recapitulate and *reclaim*. For example: recapitulating our anger at opening the mail box and finding bills, may open the memory of a bully from first grade. This bully used to say, "time to pay your bills," which meant our lunch money, but also made us angry. Recapitulating the bully can lead us to other emotionally charged events that we can then recapitulate as well. As we *locate* emotionally significant events, we can *release* the energy that is *insisting we become activated*.

Clearing up old emotional influences allows us to further reclaim a working relationship with our emotions. A phone becomes useless if everything is sent directly to voicemail. A voicemail box that is loaded with important messages from the past cannot just be erased. We must go through the messages to find out what *is* going on. With an empty "emotional voicemail box," we often have the confidence to pick up the emotional phone when it rings. Instead of letting our emotional messages go to the voicemail box of suppressed memories.

Learning to hear the "personalized ring tones" of different emotions, helps to prepare us for the "emotional phone call" when it comes. The process of recapitulation teaches us how to be an impartial observer of our internal processes. Observing impartially allows us a clear view of what we are doing and saying to ourselves *inside* our minds. Clarity of internal vision can reveal motivations we were unaware of.

With enough practice we eventually feel a tiny little notification that is: anger, happiness, sadness, frustration, etc. Emotion becomes a simple indicator, letting us know our attitude is about to change and which direction it will be heading. Instead of waiting until our needs become an emergency, we will notice our present path does not lead to a positive outcome. Once we notice we are not heading in a positive direction, we can *choose* a different path that is positive.

Most of us have met someone who seemed to be in complete control of their emotions, never truly upset by outside events. Not an emotionless person, quite the contrary. This person always seemed to come up with a new plan or new energy, even after what most would consider a setback. It seemed like they always had more positivity and energy for the next moment. I am **not** sure we can, or should, get to the point where *nothing* touches us emotionally. However, I *do* believe we should be able to *decide* when emotion is going to benefit us and when it is not.

Reality is change. Our environment does things to us; the definition of life dictates we do things back. The definition of life does *not* say life complains or throws a fit about reality. Taking charge of our past allows us to take charge of our present. When we take charge of our present situation, we end up in charge of our life. The more we answer the call and take the necessary action, the better we will like ourselves and the more others will desire our presence.

Control is something everyone wants but often those *seeking* control, receive only frustration. **The only thing we have any hope of controlling is our selves**. Most do not even have control of themselves.

In codependent relationships, we are taught to rely on *others* to anticipate and appease *our* needs. Those reared in codependence believe they are being mistreated, If needs arise that others are unwilling to meet. Codependence is a false reality where everyone is responsible for taking care of *everyone else's* needs, instead of everyone taking responsibility for *their own* needs.

Children rely exclusively on others for their wants, needs and desires. As we mature, we become more complex in our desires, needs and the ways we make our decisions. Figuring ourselves out and keeping the subconscious happy is no easy puzzle. (see: Raising Ourselves) Maturity is the *act* of *taking responsibility* for acquiring, accomplishing and solving our own wants, needs and desires. The act of expecting others to decide what is best for us, instead of learning to do it for ourselves, is a perpetual self imposed childhood.

Often in moments of emotional pressure, we feel as though we are pulled in several directions at once. The mind is like a day care center for all the parts of us that still behave like children. When we are upset, stressed, or distracted, we are dealing with our "internal daycare center." If we just ground, scold and spank our way through our problems, we are creating future stress for ourselves.

Releasing the energy stored in our past will slow the storm inside us to a gentle breeze. Once the turmoil of a troubled past is drained of its power, we can easily listen to our internal concerns.

Everyone who experiences oppression will eventually *rebel* against the *oppressing force*, even if the oppression comes from *our selves*. Many parents of grown children can testify that grounding, scolding, and spanking only teach children to wait till those who oppress are distracted or absent to "misbehave." On the other hand, if we choose to *accept* each need, urge, and pressure we feel about our situation, we can come closer to reaching a decision that will actually make us happy.

When we are stressed out, sad, tired, drained, etc. emotions and instincts appear to influence more of our actions. The fact is: emotions and instincts are *always* trying to influence our actions. It is easier to give in to our more primitive side when we are stressed out, sad, tired etc. Noticing our personal process is our opportunity to come up with a better program. Many of us just push these emotions down or "send them to their room," instead of *watching* the process to recognize *why* we are feeling this way.

Emotions arise when we have an issue with our environment. Emotions and instincts are the guidelines we use to figure out what we need to do in order to be happy. The energy stored in our experiences must be released, so we can use it to power our ability to pursue our passions. All our urges and desires can be appeased legally if we learn what they truly are. Instead of jumping on the "bus called anger," see if the bus will take us where we want to go. As we reclaim our past and the energy from our experiences, decision making becomes easier, and our decisions appease more of our wants, needs and desires.

The calmest people I have ever met live their lives in acceptance. Alcoholics Anonymous advocates the use of acceptance in one of its famous teachings, the serenity prayer. The serenity prayer asks us to: "*Change* the things we can, *accept* the things we cannot change, and to *know* the difference." I believe the message is correct, but I choose to use it as follows. First we need to, *know* what is real. Ask questions, experiment, discover what is changeable and what is not, find the truth. Once we have an opinion worth hearing, we have *accepted* what is possible. Then we can be efficient with our resources when we decide to *Change* the things we can.

"Who you are becomes more a description centered in the here and now, and less a story about your life." ~Blanton, Brad (1994) *Radical Honesty*, Pg. 76

RAISING OURSELVES

"I am not sure what I am, I just know there is something dark in me, and I hide it. I certainly don't talk about it, but it's there always, this dark passenger. And when he's driving I feel, alive, half sick with the thrill of complete wrongness. I don't fight him, I don't want to. He's all I've got, Nothing else could love me, not even... especially not me. Or is that just a lie the dark passenger tells me? Because lately there are these moments when I feel connected to something else... someone. It's like the mask is slipping and things... people... who never mattered before are starting to matter, and it scares the hell out of me."

(Dexter 2007)

To get a handle on all the internal currents pushing and pulling us this way and that, we must do something very few are taught to do. Many of us believe that people are either too simple, or too complicated to figure out. In short, deciding *not* to think about what, how and why we are inspired and/or driven to do all of the things we do.

There is an animal inside us. This animal does not speak a verbal language and does not understand money or time. This animal understands the present moment. Food, sex, territory and dominance, (not domination) are the foundation for the animal. On top of this foundation is emotion, the need for praise, love, social interaction, laughter as well as negative emotions like anger, jealousy and others. (Triune Brain Theory: Caine, Renate Nummela and Geoffrey Caine. (1990)

We watch the animal from the time we have our first thoughts. Some of us develop a separation between the watcher who speaks to us in words (the committee, internal dialog, etc.) and the animal with all of its various feelings and non verbal inclinations. The speaker (logic, ego, mind) thinks it can control the animal (instinct and emotion or body and spirit) and it will often use the same method its parents used to control it.

This animal is the one who wants candy, possessions, sex and all the rest RIGHT NOW, regardless of the consequences. Like a new puppy, we must teach it how to be patient and how to earn what it wants. We must also show this animal unconditional regard. We must prove every time we interact with it, we have its best interests at heart. We must prove to the animal we are willing to go, do and be all we must, to make good on our promises. If we don't take care of the animal, peeing on the carpet, chewing up the sofa, and getting into the garbage manifest themselves when the animal takes over.

Most of us have experienced the animal's influence when we were putting an unfair amount of pressure on ourselves, or being pressured by others. The animal was so full of anger that it overflowed; we said some things we regret, threw something through a window, or broke a relationship. We knew the trouble we would cause for ourselves, how terrible we would feel after, but we simply *could not help* behavior like:

binge eating, friendship breaking, tantrums, and heading to the local bar to look for a fight.

When we lie to the animal, it learns not to *trust us*. How many of us have felt betrayed by our body at one time or another? The best way to end up in a sour mood is to ignore the animal. When we are hungry, we must acknowledge the hunger and promise food soon. Everything we do must *show* the animal that we are hunting down some food. If we say we will eat soon but do not, we have just taught the animal we cannot be trusted. If we have to go to the bathroom and wish the pressure to ease for just a moment, so we don't have an accident, be *honest* with the animal and it *will* work with us. The animal is our body trying to communicate all of its issues. The animal will make us feel better than we thought we could, if we show it the respect and care we would like from others.

As we learn our personal favorite internal obsessions, we must speak to this part of ourselves as though it were our beloved 4 year old child. Use words so we know the deal we are making, but understand we are talking to the animal. Like instructing a puppy, strong words can sometimes be necessary. However, there must *always* be love and respect, or we will raise ourselves as a dysfunctional child or an angry dog.

There is more than one perspective in each of us. Part of growing up and claiming maturity is finding a compromise between all our internal perspectives. Learning to understand our emotions and instincts, will go a long way to making our body feel good and function properly. In order to be at peace with ourselves, it stands to reason that our different perspectives must learn to work together. Learn to love the inner animal, make our body and spirit (instincts and emotions) our strongest allies in living a long and enjoyable life.

"Growing up is hard, and it's supposed to be, you're not like anyone else, you're Dean, and you're the best Dean." ~McCulloch, McCulloch & Hammer, 2013

EMOTION IS THE ALARM

We have many different emotions that are all "a *part*" of us, but not always *us*. Sometimes emotions inspire us to feel like someone *else* is causing our experiences to happen *to* us; as if we are merely a passenger in our own lives.   Our emotions and instincts are: a basic nonverbal communication process between our cerebral cortex and the *older parts* (emotions and instincts) of the brain.

When we listen to our animal (emotions and instincts) and work with them, we often feel like we are "in control of ourselves." When we resist, ignore, or try to deny our animal, it slowly becomes angry. Anger is an emotion that is inspired by our instinct to protect ourselves and our territory. Many of our primary "emotions" are inspired by instinct. Instinct is concerned with protecting our lives and our territory.

Anger is the animal telling us when we *need* to *say* "no," to ourselves or someone else. The animal also tells us, when we *should hear* "no," from someone or something outside of us. When we feel anger, we must *change* the moment or *change* ourselves. The animal is the key to personal evolution. Every time we are *feeling*, the animal is telling us something in our environment, or in our personality, needs to change. Rising emotional pressure means there is a "no" that needs to be *said* or *heard*, to relieve the pressure. We must stand up for our feelings in order to prevent emotional escalation from clouding our vision.

Getting angry is wonderful; it is *the* force of change. The issue with anger arises when we become angry about a situation we *cannot* change. Anger becomes the enemy when we cannot easily tell the difference between what is changeable and what is not. When we make no changes and just try to bury anger, the anger resurfaces more powerfully the next time we encounter the same situation. Anger needs change like someone who is drowning needs air.

Anger tells us to change the world or change ourselves. The change in ourselves can be as simple as walking away, to as complicated as allowing our 13 year old daughter to go to the school dance with a partner we know is going to break her heart. She must learn how to judge the people she wishes to date in order to protect herself. As a father I must learn to accept: the best protection for my daughter is *not* my anger at her choices, but my *acceptance* that I will *not always be there to protect her*. It is my job to help her learn how to survive *without me*.

Anxiety is the emotional energy that builds up when we are avoiding a decision. Anxiety can also build when we are in an unfamiliar situation. When we are unsure of what to do, we are stuck in indecision. In new situations, we do not know exactly how to navigate and get through them, because they are unknown to us. When confronted with unfamiliar things, it is important to know the *anxiety* we feel, is *energy* to "get the job done," whatever "the job" may be. As we make decisions in new environments, we become comfortable and familiar where we were once nervous.

When walking into our favorite beverage shop, on our way to work or an important meeting, we see that the line is somewhat long, and we only have five extra minutes. Anyone who is ready to feel some anxiety, will start to feel it in the situation described above. The energy from anxiety is informing us that we need to make a decision. "No beverage today," or "as long as it takes," are two decisions we can easily go back and forth between. Anxiety continues to build while we desperately try to figure out if we will allow ourselves to wait for our treat, or pass on the treat to make sure we are on time.

Fear comes in through the darkness. We usually only fear something we know little or nothing about. Skydivers will tell you skydiving is one of the most exciting, exhilarating experiences they have ever felt. Those of us who have never tried skydiving, will have some fear attached to the idea of jumping out of a perfectly good airplane.

Facing our fears is all about bringing the light of understanding into the darkness of the unknown. Facing our fear does not always require jumping out of "the airplane of the known," into the "free fall of the unknown." Educating ourselves about our fears is a way to face them. Do some research, talk to those who have experienced our fear; there will be time to jump later. Choosing not to educate ourselves, while living with fear, turns the energy of fear into a depression which states: **"I can never choose to overcome this fear."**

Depression can come from many sources. Unused emotional energy turns into depression. When we become angry at someone or something and we do not change ourselves or the environment, the energy is stored inside us as depression. When we are unable to make a decision, for example: to go or not to go to a party, the anxiety from indecision is stored as depression. When we spend all our time alone, and have no one (people or animals) to interact with, our social energy is stored as depression. When we eat food that does not nourish us properly, do not eat enough, or eat too much we are punishing our body, which becomes depressed. When we do not get enough sleep, or sleep too much we become depressed. If we allow others to manipulate or use us, we lose self esteem and become (you guessed it) depressed.

Depression is the catch all for taking care of our wants, needs and desires. If we are depressed, we need to check the easy fixes first. If we are hungry or stuffed, lonely or over socialized, tired, on the fence of indecision, or resisting reality, we can have a bite to eat or stop eating, call a friend, take a nap, make a decision, or accept some reality. All the emotional energy we *do not use in the moment* is stored, in our body as depression.

~Try This~

Create a list for a happy life. The list should include what we would like to experience in our lives. Here is an example of a happy life list:

Things I want in my life:

- Kindness
- Decisiveness
- Honesty
- Charity
- Backbone
- Positivity
- Happiness

Every time we are faced with an unfamiliar situation or a new decision, it can be an opportunity to look for the things on our list. We can find these things in ourselves or in those around us. Our list will be the clues we use to guide us in choosing who we wish to have in our lives, as well as who we wish to be ourselves.

The alarm we call emotion is here to inform us something is going on *right now*, that *must* be addressed. When we do not deal with emotions immediately, "answer the alarm," we are storing emotional energy *in* the experience. Emotional energy stored in our experiences, adds itself to *every new* experience of the same type. For example: held back anger is still inside us; new anger will bring up the energy of the old anger. This emotionally charged experience may stay quiet for a while, but when similar emotions are stimulated, they will escalate unrealistically.

In order to force a change in our reality, emotional energy will continue to build over the days, months and years. Emotional energy will eventually become too powerful to contain. Once we have stored all the energy we can, the energy will explode in an unrealistic escalation of emotion. Our emotions *will lash out* for change, justice, fairness, respect and so on.

Every emotionally charged situation is a lesson waiting to be learned. Until we learn the lesson, we will continue to experience similar situations, which will continue to activate us. The more we are activated *without learning our lesson*, "change the world, or change our self," the more emotional pressure we are storing *in* ourselves. Learning the lesson is simply changing what we can, and acceptance of what we cannot change or predict. The future is not written, so let's keep our emotions in the present.

We can take drugs to forget this anger, to mask that emotion, but if we do, we are not maintaining the communication which is *necessary* to maintain happiness and congruence with ourselves, for the rest of our lives. Without honest communication with ourselves, we are like a codependent teen, more concerned with appearances than results. What we do and how we feel, are not as important to us as what we believe others think of us.

We must develop an honest relationship with our emotions, by *saying* only what we *know will* happen. For example: "I am going to get out of bed and take a shower." Save the hopes and dreams for affirmations and visualizations. For example: "I am going to build a pocket fusion reactor." Speak them to ourselves as motivation *and do them*. Let the desires we want to make a reality, echo inspiration in our head; do not speak of them casually to others, *take action*. For example: when we are not making enough money, we can tell everyone how hard it is to only make the money we make. We can tell our friends we are going to demand a raise, *or we can go* to the source, like a boss, or a business plan, and see if there is room for extra earning.

Emotions are an intimately personal communication with oneself. Emotions often inspire a statement from our logic, regarding the change we *think* we want like the fusion reactor. Many people share this statement with others at the moment of conception, during the emotional charge. I believe statements like this are for *ourselves*, to be used as motivation for change, not to be shared in words but in actions.

When we share our emotional inspiration in words over and over again, without taking action, we are "blowing off steam;" releasing the energy we need to motivate our deeds. When we do not know how to deal with our emotions, blowing off steam is one of the few ways to avoid an emotional meltdown, outburst, tantrum etc. Sometimes we must put up with situations that we would like to change in order to survive. In these situations the ability to blow off steam can make life easier to handle.

We must always remember to attempt to use our emotional energy properly, and only blow off steam as a safety valve. Blowing off steam will relieve the emotional pressure for a short time, but most of the emotional energy is still inside, waiting to come out. Emotional energy will not stay hidden forever and if we don't do something, the animal *will*.

When emotions are held back, the pressure builds until they explode on the next person or event which inspires that emotion. A close relationship with our emotions, allows us to deal with them *immediately*. An active, moment by moment, awareness of our internal processes, will lead us to a method of using the emotional energy we feel, efficiently and effectively. When we share unsolicited emotions, we are releasing the power stored in those emotions. The emotional energy we release would otherwise be used as the power to *make* our much needed change. Dealing with emotions as they arise, is a way to relieve stress, anxiety, anger etc. *before* they become too much for us to handle.

Every day is your birthday, there is so much to discover, but you must look in the present. ~Jesse Anzini

THE SECURITY BLANKET
CALLED ANGER

When something in our world appears to be hurting us, or causing us loss (P. Dobransky) we become angry. This anger is the energy that says, "This is the only time this is going to happen to me!" Or, "I will never let this happen again!" This is the energy *given* to us to make the necessary changes. Unfortunately, most of us use this anger to break things, including relationships.

Anger is often used to keep people at a distance. Anger can be used to give us a time of rest from having to negotiate and compromise with others. Unfortunately negotiation and compromise are some of the most powerful tools in teaching us about ourselves. The lessons learned while negotiating with others can be used to negotiate with *ourselves*. The requests and expectations of others can be unreasonable, unethical and sometimes impossible, so can our internal expectations. Inside or out, tools are tools.

We have all been angry at one time or another, for one reason or another. I can remember times when I was angry at people for doing things that I do myself. Noticing where we are hypocrites can be a difficult pill to swallow. I had been angry quite often, over various issues and I suddenly knew, "I have been doing many of the same things that make me angry at others, for as long as I can remember." We must *accept* those parts of ourselves we were *taught to look down upon* and learn to live with them. This acceptance translates perfectly, whether we are dealing with ourselves or dealing with others.

The realization of personal hypocrisy was a fork in the road for me. I chose to stop doing all of the things that made me mad at others, so I could *feel justified* in being angry at them. The plan to hold myself to a strict code of conduct made me feel good about judging others harshly. I was better than others and therefore, could treat them like dirt. I was a judgmental little punk, so this plan worked great, except for one little snag. I was still angry and now I was becoming very skilled at getting angrier and angrier.

I spent several years of my life in this stage. It took more than one angry outburst to open my eyes to the fact that I *did not want* to be angry anymore. I wanted to be relaxed, at peace with myself and the world around me. I had to go back to that fork in the road and *choose* a different path.

This time, I chose to accept that I could not change others. However, I still found myself angry at others for doing things I did not *allow myself* to do. This helped me realize I was not angry at them. I was angry at myself for trying to be someone I was not. I was still trying to measure up to some 'ideal man" I had created in my head, when I was reading comic books at 13 years old. Since I *knew* everything at the age of 13 (don't we all?) I had never bothered to update my image of the "ideal man." Unfortunately the ideal person I was attempting to turn myself into, did not satisfy my basic psychological and physical needs as a human being.

When we feel hurt, or as if we have lost something, we become angry. Anger is the energy used for change, we become angry when we need to stop hurt, or end loss. To deal with anything, we must first become familiar with it. In order to become familiar with or anger, we must be able to *watch* it critically.

Use observing ego to step *outside* of *emotion* and *watch* the *process* of anger. Become interested in when and how often the anger appears. "Wow, this is the 3rd time I have gotten angry today…" Make a game of anger by keeping score. "I was only angry 5 times today. Yesterday, I was angry 16 times…" Make lists of all the crazy things that we let make us angry. "I was angry at the vending machine, my co-worker, my cell phone, several cars as I drove to and from work, an automatic door at the grocery store and two stoplights!" It is easy to see the comedy in these situations.

Are we dealing with reality in our anger, or are we dealing with a fantasy? Did we try to predict the future of how events would unfold, and when they did not turn out the way we wanted, we became angry? Were we creating a fantasy and then resisting when reality set in?

Gambling our emotions on a future event is like "anger layaway." "If they don't call me next I will be pissed," "If the light turns red…" "If they say one more thing…" "If I have to tell them one more time…" When we make these kinds of statements, even to ourselves, we are writing emotional checks. If things do not go as planned, we will cash them in for anger.

Predicting the future can be considered a type of emotional gambling. When driving in the car, "I bet ten emotional dollars I will have an open road. I bet twenty emotional dollars I will be able to drive fast." If the bets come true, we *feel* happy from the returns on gambled emotions. However, if there was a car that prevented the bet from coming true, the *loss we feel* is the same amount of emotional energy we originally gambled on our ability to predict the future.

Here is an example of the process. There are obviously many ways to view the following event, here are three possibilities.

- "The green car cut me off. I wanted to drive faster. The green car is blocking what was once an open road. Therefore, the green car made me angry."
- "The green car pulled into the lane in front of me. I had planned to drive faster. My plan was denied by the green car's actions. The green car made me lose the ability to execute my plan. The inability to follow my plan made me angry."
- **The reality is**: "The green car pulled into the lane ahead of me. The option to drive faster requires an open road. Therefore, the option of driving faster is not available."

One way to avoid emotional gambling is to stay out of the future and the past. The only place we can make decisions is in the present. "Is the road still clear? Visual scan says no. Maintain current speed, or match speed with the leading car."

When we feel emotion starting to rise, we must be *aware* of our *part* in the situation. Shooting from the hip is how we will learn to shoot from the hip. Emotion demands immediate action. Use anger for what it is: **Automatic Natural Guidance** for **Energy Redirection.**

CRITICS

I agree that some people could have more tact in delivering criticism. However, if any one can say something and hurt us, we have some work to do on ourselves. If we know who we are and we genuinely like ourselves, nothing anyone says should be able to get through to our feelings. Some criticisms are offered simply because we happen to look to others for approval. Most criticism delivered with emotional content is projection. Some criticism can even be helpful.

The other person has every right to believe what they want, because so do we. Criticism hurts *when we believe it* to be true. A lack of *confidence* in any area of our lives *is simply* a lack of *exploration*. We must become aware of the areas where *we* have doubt. Where we have doubt, there is room to do some personal research. Find out which decision or point of view we respect regarding the criticism. The *respect* we have for a certain point of view or decision *will become confidence* in ourselves, if we adopt this point of view or decision as our own.

For example when someone says we are too short or too tall, too loud or too quiet, they are voicing their opinion. If we like our appearance, the first two criticisms are laughable. However, most of us have been teased about our appearance and felt the sting of criticism. Our behavior is no different if we are in command of ourselves; we are behaving how we have chosen to behave.

If we want others to be nice to us because we are *fragile,* we will spend most of our time as a victim. If everyone we meet in the world is responsible for our feelings, our life will be a constant rollercoaster of changing emotions. Expecting others to be aware of all our feelings is unrealistic. Many of us are strangers to ourselves and we are around us all day; how is someone who really is a stranger, supposed to anticipate our issues or needs? We must show others our boundaries by saying no when the answer is no. Once we start looking to ourselves for approval, the criticisms of others are no longer an attack but an offer of discussion.

When we are children we let others influence us. The influence of others is a big part of learning to be human and "fit in." As we get older, doing as others advise us will hopefully teach us: there is only one person who has the right to make decisions for us. It's not our mom and it's not our favorite uncle. These people may be respectable, they may make good decisions, they may believe they have our best interests at heart. However, they haven't lived our life; they don't see through our eyes and they don't know us as well as *we* should *know ourselves.*

In the end we must reap the rewards or suffer the consequences of the things we do. The ability to make good and timely decisions is learned by making not so good and not so timely decisions. The faster we start making our own decisions, the faster our decision making skills improve.

Criticism tells us two things: how others choose to view what we do, and how they view themselves. If we have ourselves and others best interests at heart, which means we are kind and fair with others and ourselves, there is absolutely every reason to believe in ourselves. If we believe in ourselves, what power does criticism have over us? Criticisms only have the power we give them, the power of doubt.

Philosophical note:

If anyone ever says something to me that isn't to my liking, I laugh; because either it's a joke, or they need some therapy for trying to take their dysfunctional mental processes out on me. Mean people don't exist in my world. There are nice people, there are comedians and some of the comedians need help.

Criticism may be the public expression of a need for personal growth. People, who need help handling their reality, lash out to be educated. When someone is unable to transform anger into change, they turn the anger inward and it becomes depression. Depression can lead to passive-aggressive behavior, of which criticism is one.

Perhaps criticism is the symptom of someone stuck in dissatisfaction. The same way a drifting lifeboat passenger uses flairs to signal a passing ship. What would a ship captain do if a life boat occupant refused to leave the lifeboat? Is it up to the Capitan to convince the castaway to leave the lifeboat? We cannot save anyone else; we can only help them to save themselves.

"The greatest of teachers won't hesitate, to leave you there by yourself chained to fate" (Kowalczyk, 1994)

REFLECTION

The concept of projection (Freud, 1890) is one of many tools to help with perspective, acceptance and self discovery. I remember being baffled by such questions as: "how do I find out who I am, what makes me "me," is there really a "me," or am I just a genetically directed collection of personality traits selected from everyone I have known?"

~Try this~

- List three people you admire and three you do not.
- List three things about each person on your list, that make them admirable or not.

The first time this test is done is usually the most eye opening. Come up with a few answers before reading on. Common psychology proposes the answers to the above questions are "projections." The traits that are *not* admirable are things we do not like about *ourselves*. The *admirable* traits are things we *like* about ourselves. Exploring our positives and negatives can tell us quite a bit about our shadow. Our shadow is that which is not an integrated part of our consciousness, but resides within our mind. The traits revealed by this exercise are our personal strengths or lessons, areas where we can excel, blossom, learn and grow.

I like to take this test a step further and propose the traits reveled via projection may be things we were *taught* to admire or dislike. Try the exercise again in a few weeks, also try to forget that we are looking into ourselves and be honest about the likes and dislikes. Some of the admiration may stop inspiring after only a small amount of exploration. We soon find ourselves admiring new traits we may not have admired in the beginning of our search. New abilities we feel inspired to improve are proof we and the world are changing and so is the path ahead.

Social training available from our peer group can influence what we value and admire. Pursuing our inspiration can help us find and define our path. Sometimes what we find is only the reflection of the world we were trained to seek. We must pursue our inspiration to its limits. *To find* deeper and more *authentic* inspiration, *we* must *surpass* or *break through* the limitations of our training.

When we are riding or driving in a car, we will often make predictions about other drivers. Perhaps the driver of that large pick up is a bully, the Volkswagen has timid people inside and the Hummer barely sees the other cars as they own the road. We do not know how these other people feel, but if they cut us off they must be angry, if they are constantly riding their breaks they are timid and if they are cutting through traffic at dangerous speed, they are self centered jerks.

All of the previous examples are examples of projection. If someone is pregnant and going into labor, there might be a bit of speeding to shorten the trip to the hospital. People are often running late for appointments of all sorts. There are plenty of reasons for people to behave the way they do, but they are not always the reasons we think.

Children of divorced parents often blame themselves for the break up. A family or peer group's constant attention to find fault and inadequacy, can lay the groundwork for a person to believe *they* are the reason things go wrong. "It must be something *I* did…" A lack of honest sharing with our children, parents, peers etc. leads to all sorts of misconceptions and misunderstandings.

When a person's behavior changes and we *know* something is "wrong," but no one will say what it is, we are left to make up our own answers. When trying to figure out the behaviors and actions of others, the answers *we* make up are often more about *ourselves* than about *them*. *Knowing* our own issues and being able to *see* our own process will help us discern the truth of our reality.

Whenever we think someone is angry, we are recognizing some of *our own* anger in them. The expressions of others may mean what we think they mean, or they may have a different meaning behind them. We are most ready to recognize behaviors we have the most experience with.

- Angry people often think everyone is angry.

- Depressed people often think everyone is either depressed, or depressing.

- Practical jokers often think everyone is in on the joke, or are trying to play their own joke.

Projection works in several directions. The judgments of others are often only a projection from the person *judging*. We are all ready to recognize our own issues in other people; the people we meet are mirrors, showing us all the things *we* have issues with. When we become emotionally activated by someone's behavior, it is time to ask ourselves how often *we* behave in the exact same way. Recognizing when we are being activated shows us we have an issue *within* ourselves that is unresolved. The unresolved issue is a conflict in our programming. Those we learn from do not always agree and if we absorb their lessons, we absorb their conflict.

We were taught or we learned to disapprove of certain behaviors. We notice someone acting in a way we were taught to disapprove of and the anger, frustration or disappointment we feel may be *pointed* at the person who is "misbehaving." However the anger, frustration or disappointment we feel toward the other, is fueled by *urges* we were taught to suppress or ignore in *ourselves*.

We were taught many of the things we *want* to do are "wrong." Some of the urges we feel may be non productive, but many are simply misused or misunderstood. We must do our own research to find out which parts of our *shadow* (all that is "wrong" with us) can be used *positively*. Here are some examples of useful tools from our shadow.

- **Selfishness** has a bad reputation, but is actually something every fully functional person has a handle on. We must selfishly protect our health, happiness and wellbeing. Often when protecting ourselves, we are accused of being selfish. However, without this "selfish" protection, we are quickly drained of self esteem and then easily taken advantage of.

- **Manipulation** is another behavior with a bad reputation. Convincing your children that the poisonous chemicals under the sink are not as fun as the play dough, is a form of manipulation. Asking a "stay at home" friend to ride the bus into the city with you for safety, is a way to manipulate a homebody into getting out of their house.

- We all have some experience with **lies**. When we look for something to label a "lie," we only see negative, detrimental, painful examples. Creating analogies or stories to convey meanings, morals and rules to live by are what we refer to as fiction. Fiction, being made of fantasy, also fits the definition of a "lie."

Respect, trust and love to name a few, are examples of social currency we use to trade, deal, and interact fairly with others. We must respect, love or trust ourselves **before** *we will* **let** *anyone else* pay us these complements. If we do not believe we deserve love, money or success, we will not trust those who try to give them to us. If we think we are unlovable, those who show us love are seen as gold diggers, manipulators, con artists, foolish, uneducated etc. In short, anyone who gives us what we do not think we deserve, must have an ulterior motive, or there must be something wrong with them.

Self exploration is the only way we will learn who we are. Testing ourselves on a regular basis can tell us where we are in our personal evolution. Recognize patterns of projection; where are we seeing clearly and where are we seeing *ourselves* in *another* person's behavior? Where are we allowing *others* to tell us who *we* are? Where are we afraid to flex the muscles of our shadow? When do we give ourselves permission to receive all the gifts life has to give us? When do we *allow* ourselves to *be* the amazing person we are: evolving, growing and becoming a better version of ourselves?

THE GIFT OF NO

When I was first developing my ability to make friends, I was told it was best to be "nice." I was also taught that when someone asks you for something, in order to be "nice," the only answer a nice person has is yes, or an amazing "excuse" to get out of saying "yes." I was also taught that if I said "no," I might lose good relations with the person I denied. If someone asked me to help them move, I would *have* to say "yes," even when I *knew* I could not hold up my end of the bargain.

Like many other young boys, I was brought up to do everything for everyone. I was taught service to others was the definition of accommodation. Service and accommodation were the tools I was taught to use, to make friends and be a "good person." It took most of my young life to learn that this is how to be a victim and give away all your resources. "No" was my protection from being used, yet I was taught "No," was the language of selfishness, friendlessness and even irresponsibility. My job on this earth as a "good person," was to say "yes" to everyone who had the ability to ask.

Saying "yes" quickly became a full time job. I had made many "friends," but all I was doing every day, was what *everyone else* needed done. I started being unavailable when it became time to do the deed I had agreed to, then unavailable for the question. Instead of learning to say "no," I learned to be cold and flaky. I had so thoroughly been trained in the use of "yes," that being cold and flaky was easier, in my mind, than the simple act of saying "no."

For me, the first thing I had to do was make the word "No" an option. I would imagine myself saying "no" to that person, not imagining how they might react, just looking at me in a mental mirror and seeing myself say the word. The simple image of myself saying "no," was not effective for all situations. I would also use an image of myself, as a seven year old child, stomping my foot and saying "NO!!" in a near fit or tantrum. This practice made the situations almost funny and far less stressful.

Sometimes the best way to learn a lesson is to ask the question I was taught next. How do I feel when someone tells me yes, but later backs out on the deal, or is simply a no show? It hurt my feelings and sometimes left me stuck in situations that were not easy to get myself out of. Reversing the roles is a good way to start examining a decision to see if it is good for *all* parties involved.

The ability to tell someone "no," when the answer is "no," is often quite an effort for those who were trained to do only as we were told. This is one of the first steps to proper boundary function, responsibility, respectability and honest relations with others. Whenever we say anything other than the truth, we are giving that person a flawed reality to work with, and we also lower their chances of making a good, effective decision.

"No" is the word used to enforce ones boundaries. Everything we have is protected by the word "no." When we do not, or feel we cannot use the word "no," we are voluntarily giving away what is ours. Our resources include things like time, effort, expertise, self esteem etc. as well as material things like money, tools and real-estate. We must be aware of the resources *we give* to our relationships every time we pass up a chance to use the word "no."

To let it slide or not to let it slide? Every time we let something in a relationship "slide," there was a "*no*" that needed to be said. Each "no" we do not say is a straw ("camel's back" pg. 34) in the anger (energy for change) bundle. When someone does or says something that gets under our skin, many of us were trained to let it "slide." Letting things "slide" is also commonly referred to as, "bottling up our emotions or anger." To be a whole person, we have to deal with *all* aspects of our self; this means activities and food as well as thoughts and feelings.

We have all experienced a relative or friend who could not hear the word "no." "Can I get you something to drink?" they would say for the fifth time. Then they would begin listing every beverage in the house, in an attempt to change the "No thank you," into a "Sure." This is an example of somewhat harmless manipulation, but manipulation none the less. Since we didn't want to listen to this person describe all the beverages in their house, either we gave up and choose from the list, or we asked them for "…a glass of shut the hell up about something to drink already."

Sneaking through our boundaries is one way people can gain access to our resources without our consent. People who cannot hear the word "no," use manipulative statements in an attempt to reach through our boundaries and "push our buttons." When someone is able to say or do something that does not touch us physically in any way, but still manages to activate us, that person just snuck through a hole in our boundaries and pushed a button. When people are able to activate us emotionally, instinctually or logically, the fact that we became activated *tells* us we have some repair work to do on our boundaries.

People who push our buttons may not be the most fun to be around, but they do make us aware of holes in our boundaries. People who continually attempt to manipulate us have been referred to as: "petty tyrants" by Carlos Castaneda (1984). Petty tyrants actually help us zero in on our boundary holes and once we patch them, test our repair job.

We all know how it feels to be manipulated and have our buttons pushed. When someone is able to control us by activating our emotions, the process does not feel good because it causes a loss of self esteem. Every time someone other than us controls our actions without our consent, they are exploiting a hole in our boundaries. The holes in our boundaries allow self esteem to leak out (Paul Dobransky). Whenever we discover a hole in our boundaries, it is important to *close the hole*. By closing holes in our boundaries, we retain our self esteem and retain control of our actions.

Often we do not see an opportunity to say "no" to "button pushing." Button pushing is not always formed as a question. Here are some examples of statements that are looking to sneak past our boundaries and *control* or *manipulate* us:

- "I know it's not your favorite thing to do, but I need someone to watch the kids." **Translation:** "Do what I tell you whenever I call." **The no:** "How dare you say I don't like to babysit my grandchildren?!"

- "You are so sensitive." **Translation:** "You just have to put up with my rotten behavior." **The no:** "No, I am not being *sensitive*; I am unwilling to put up with your emotional games." Or "I happen to enjoy the company of people who respect themselves enough to respect others."

- "Everyone is doing it, don't be such a downer" (often used after a *no* has been issued.) **Translation:** "Whenever I snap my fingers for entertainment, you should be happy to entertain me." **The** **extended** **no:** "Entertainment is an escape from your troubles, your lack of happiness. No one can give you happiness; you must make your own."

- "You are, young/smart/strong, you should be, happy/rich/healthy." **Translation:** "You are sad/poor/sickly if you don't want to play my game." **The no:** "Those are your issues please keep them to yourself.

    Note: when the button pusher makes an equation in this way, the statement is often a projection (see Reflection) of *their* values; they must feel young to be happy, smart to be rich, strong to be healthy etc.

Some button pushing is phrased as a personal statement that contradicts our actions. I wanted to play rock and roll and I had learned respect was often given to rebellious and anti social rock musicians. I told my "mental security force" to let rebellious and antisocial beliefs, thoughts, (memes) etc. through my boundaries. I felt I needed to collect some of those memes in order to be rebellious and antisocial myself.

I once asked an older musician if he knew any songs he could teach me to play. His reply still rings in my ears, "I don't play anyone else's music; I only play music I made up myself." The older musician's statements sounded like rebellion worth respect. I used his statements to justify shunning other people's music, and thereby crippled my own ability to learn to play a musical instrument. I chose to respect the statement of this older musician because the statement had a *"**rebellion pass**,"* which my security force was told to let through my boundaries. By allowing certain statements a "pass" through my boundaries, I allowed this older musician's statement to change *my* path like I was remote controlled.

Taking note of the situation and the *activating language,* will eventually lead us to the source. Recapitulation (see: Re-Beginning) is the tool I used to release the emotion which was clouding my vision. In the musician example above, I had placed quite a bit of *emotional energy* on his statement when I let it through my boundaries. I told myself, "This belief will make me the most rebellious rock star ever. I will make a whole new kind of music, which comes solely from me."

I used recapitulation to reclaim the emotional energy which had created reverence and respect in this crippling belief. While the emotion was attached to the older musician's statement, the idea of *learning other people's music* sounded like cheating to me. Once the emotional energy was removed, a budding musician who denied themselves musical influences became obviously foolish.

Button pushing can also be a criticism, aimed at a lack of confidence, knowledge, or social behavior. We must find our power in regards to the criticism. Our power comes from understanding the reasons for our point of view. Research and acceptance of the reality we create using our education and experience, gives us confidence. Confidence in our decisions, ideals, behaviors, self worth, values, abilities etc. allows us to deflect criticisms, which may have once been able to penetrate our boundaries. (see: Critics)

Is an emotional button always worth going after? As long as someone other than ourselves can influence our behavior, we will never be the ones truly making our own decisions. When we make decisions based mostly on the influence of others, we are giving up an opportunity to develop our own decision making process. In order to have the confidence to take responsibility for larger and larger projects, we must have confidence in our ability to make good, reliable decisions. When we allow the influence of others to change our process, we are not the ones in the driver seat. If we are not driving, how can we be sure we will make it to our destination? Emotional buttons *always* require removal.

Is there a specific time we should confront the person who activates us? If someone openly scolds, browbeats, or otherwise emotionally abuses another person, it is up to the person who is treated poorly to *change* the situation, or the scolding person's behavior by saying "no."

If someone else steps in to save us, as soon as our savior is gone so is the power of our boundaries. To insure the power of our boundaries, we must power them ourselves. As soon as someone sabotages another person's situation, the person sabotaged must decide whether to defend their situation *immediately, in that moment*, or let that particular instance go *forever*. Weather we deal with the situation in the moment or not, *we* must learn what we can about our part in the situation. Taking note of the situation and our part in it will help prepare us for the next time.

If we are prideful of a thing, that *thing* has power over us. Our peers will tease us with our pride to make us strong enough to be un-phased by the things we admire. Pride is one of many keys that can open a door in our boundaries and allow others to control us. Here are some more examples of boundary holes.

In Boxing matches the competitors will often attempt to make their opponent upset. Comments regarding the weakness of an opponent's punch, or insulting statements about ones relatives, usually mothers, are used to emotionally activate the opponent.

If anger makes us stronger, why would a boxer *seek* to anger his opponent? When angry, we will often choose a path that leads to as much discomfort and pain for the one who made us angry, even when the angry choice causes *us* pain, or costs *us* resources. Strangely enough this is also known as "getting even." Even though "getting even," rarely makes us even. Anger that flows through us unchecked lowers our chances to make good decisions.

Most angry boxers lose their matches because of poor decisions.

- Punching when no target is available, using up valuable energy.

- Lowering their defenses in favor of offensive maneuvers, creating more targets for their opponent to exploit.

- Ignoring pain and damage; damaged areas do not get extra protection, allowing the opponent to cause enough damage to disable or "Knock out" the angry opponent.

I grew up as a minority, in a school filled with those from a race/culture which had a poor view of white people (my skin color). Many of the children in my school did not see me for who I was, they only saw the color of my skin. All they saw when they looked at me was every bad thing that anyone of my race had done to them, their families, peers and friends. There were those who accepted me for who I was, but many others enjoyed tormenting me as I conveniently represented all they were taught to despise. Needless to say, I was also infected (see memes) with the idea that white people are bad.

An old friend who had dealt with racism all his life asked me a question that closed my "reverse racism" boundary hole. He asked me, "Why do you feel guilty for being white, did *you* do something? What did *you* do?" With a sigh of relief, I realized I was not responsible for people being enslaved. I was not responsible for property values in minority neighborhoods. I was not responsible for overworking and underpaying migrant workers.

The gift of "no" allows us to be our authentic selves. "No" is the word that changes our reality. "No" protects us from those who would attempt to manipulate and control us. The gift of "No" allows us to choose our own path and live *our own* life. Whenever we feel overwhelmed by emotional pressure, from ourselves or others, remember **the gift of "no."**

LIFE ACCORDING TO ALGEBRA

~NOTE: NO ALGEBRA REQUIRED~

When we first learn math, we are taught that "x" represents multiplication. However, in algebra a dot represents multiplication, and "x" becomes a variable: the unknown. Algebra has been around for quite some time. Why would we continue to teach younger children that an x means multiplication, when we know algebra disagrees with this?

Algebra is simply one of the many examples in life where we have to **let go** of what we have learned in the past, in order to learn something new. A student who is able to let go of what they have learned, will find algebra quite easy indeed. The ease with which a student learns algebra also demonstrates the ability to accept the fact that *reality* is constantly changing.

Algebra is not always easy for the Ego (faith in our knowledge) to learn. As we grow and mature we collect knowledge. We are often praised for our knowledge collecting abilities when we are children, to encourage the continued collection of information. Knowledge is great for planning a trip, writing a shopping list, reciting facts and being clever. Once we feel confident in our collection of knowledge, we can often *make ourselves believe* that knowledge is the silver bullet to reach maturity, success, love, wealth, fame, happiness, enlightenment, etc.

The Ego, out of control, is the calcification of knowledge; a base or collection of knowledge that is *unwilling* to change. Knowledge becomes a tyrant I call "Calcified Ego:" prideful, boastful and arrogant. When knowledge is combined with pride *and* an unwillingness to accept **new** information, which contradicts our **current** collection of knowledge, the Ego becomes solidified, like cement made of aging facts, stopping our growth in its tracks.

The Calcified Ego becomes intoxicated with its new found power through understanding. The calcified ego will tell us our knowledge is capable of *predicting* the future, *rewriting* our past, and *controlling* emotion and instinct like well trained slaves or machines. Here are some ways we indulge the ego and help it calcify.

- Reliving past events over and over in our thoughts.
- Creating several fantasies of the future which can never all come to pass.
- Resisting reality when it does not go our way.

These are all symptoms of a Calcified Ego and its obsession with keeping us otherwise occupied, not "in the moment."

The Ego is taught each and every one of us is perfect, but misinterprets this idea to mean we no longer have to learn, grow or change. Calcified Ego is not always interested in dealing fairly with instincts and emotions. *Ego must remember its place,* as only one of **three** major influences over our body. Emotions and instincts are the older parts of our mind. The Ego, knowledge, logic and thought, must learn to communicate with the older parts. (See Raising Ourselves) A constantly changing world is a threat to the calcified Ego. Algebra is one of many things in life attempting to teach the Ego acceptance of reality (constant change) with some useful changes in our knowledge base.

Often methods that work in one situation, will not work in other situations. The knowledge that an "x" represents multiplication will continue to be useful knowledge, even though the knowledge we gain from algebra contradicts the "old" meaning of "x." Many different strategies are necessary to deal with all the tests and lessons we find in math, and in life. Instead of becoming attached to a favorite tool that will not work in all situations, we must be able to use whichever tool works best.

Another interesting relationship between algebra and the path to maturity, is the process of solving an algebraic equation. When we first see a group of numbers and letters, which need to be added and subtracted from each other, it can be intimidating. With normal math, we know we will get a number for our answer. With algebra the answer could be any combination of numbers and/or letters.

The process of working toward a long term goal is remarkably similar to solving an algebraic equation. We may not know all we will have to do to attain our final goal, but we often know the first step. Taking the first step is of vital importance. Often after we have taken the first step, the next step becomes clear to us. As we continue down this path, as long as we follow the rules, we will arrive at our solution. It is the same with long term goals. Like writing a book; it would be great if we could download all the information from our brain straight into the computer, and simply press print. The fact of the matter is we have to:

1. Do the research.

2.   Write down all the parts that are clearest to us.

3.   Organize the pieces.

4.   Clarify sections that are too short.

5.   Edit parts that are over stated.

6.   Have others proof read the rough draft.

7.   Revise by repeating steps 4, 5 and 6.

8.   Decide you are done revising.

9.   Decide how you would like to publish the book

10. …and so on…

Many are caught in an amazingly common trap when dealing with long term goals. This is *the same fear* algebra inspires; *we cannot contemplate the entire equation in our heads, so it must be too large for us.*

The entire process does not have to be done all at once. Not only does handling everything all at once feel a bit overwhelming, it is also physically impossible. We climb stairs one at a time to reach great heights, this is *exactly* the same. We eat our food one bite at a time; imagine believing we must fit a whole meal in our mouths at one time, chew it all at once, and swallow all that we will eat that evening, day, week, year… in one gulp… ?

Faith and confidence in our "knowledge," as a "tool bag," will take us step by step, along our path. Taking one step at a time will allow us to learn how to use new tools, and discover which tool is the right one for the job.

Keep adding new tools and we will always be ready to find another tool. Collecting tools that work for us keeps the Ego adapting and changing with reality. With few tools, or only one, our path may become impassable. For more frustration in life, pick a favorite tool and risk losing the whole bag. Many long term goals *cannot* be accomplished in a single afternoon. Take a small bite out of long term goals and watch them get closer and closer.

The Reptile and Mammal (instinct and emotion, body and spirit) need goal training. The emotional and instinctual parts of the mind do not understand the concepts of algebra or long term goals. The reptile is instinctual, and used to immediate action on impulse or reflex. The mammal acts on feeling and emotion, which are known to fluctuate and respond to outside stimulation. The conscious mind must present goals with these factors in mind, so as not to confuse the reptile, and overwhelm the mammal.

Breaking long term goals into short term accomplishments satisfies the instant gratification needs of the reptile centers of the mind. Adding self praise to these short term accomplishments appeases the emotional stroking needs of the mammal part of the mind. Presenting goals in this fashion allows the different parts of the mind to work in harmony toward the desired goal.

Here is an example of goal training when deciding to adopt a weekly workout routine. Many of the things we do to "work out," can seem like punishment. To keep the reptile and mammal on track, make each part of the process a reason for celebration, even if we only celebrate on the inside. Do a little song and dance when we find our workout mat or our weights.

Indulge in a small treat and dwell in its sweetness as we watch our workout show for the first time. Think of how sweet it will be to be fit the first time we work out. Take a nice, *relaxing* shower after our first work out. Make sure to verbalize how awesome we are for accomplishing our first step toward a more fit body. For example: "I am so awesome, I may not have wanted to do it, but I did it and it will only get easier!" and so on.

Many of the ideas shared in this book come from vastly different points of view. Some of the ideas in this book will contradict each other, but *every* piece of knowledge can be a useful tool. As long as we remember our knowledge is simply a bag of tools, we can ***choose*** the right tool for the job. We can chop down a tree with a shovel, but wouldn't it be easier to trade in our shovel for an axe? Calcified Ego *will* limit our choices and without the right tool for the job, we may not be able to solve the next equation life presents us with.

WHO WANTS TO LIVE FOREVER?

When one embraces the philosophical idea that who we are today, *would* not and *could* not be possible without all those who influenced us, one begins to glimpse immortality. All those in our lives, including those who wrote the books we have read, those who helped create paper, the printing press, fire, the wheel, and everything else, influence who we are and how we see ourselves. We are all reaping the benefits of those who learned it the hard way, so we don't have to.

Immortality is the continual gain of experience, and a body able to use these experiences. One might think the question is: how do we remain young? Keeping the body from aging or rejuvenating an aging body, is a question for medical science. Perhaps the question is: how do we become old in experience faster than we do in body? Education can grant us experience and knowledge beyond our years. The ability to pass on and gain knowledge and experience, is the closest thing we have to immortality.

The question leads to the possibility that we are the reincarnation of those we follow, idolize and choose as our educators. Those we use as role models are, in a way, our previous lives. Reincarnation occurs when we accept the responsibility and burden of being a *vessel* full of all the role models we have adopted as the central philosophy of who we are.

Let us imagine for a moment we have died, leaving some record of our ideals, personality etc. Now imagine after we die, someone reads our books, studies our music, architecture, and so on. Isn't this new being going to endeavor to continue the process of refining and discovering more about their inspiration? Perhaps to one day add their discoveries to the collection of human knowledge?

Imagine finding new inspiration from someone long gone. Now imagine the more we read and discover about this person, the more new inspiration we discover. Now imagine this work becomes the primary influence in the direction of the remainder of our life. Are we not, in some ways, continuing the life of that long gone person? If they were here today, they may not be as we are, but would they not be searching as we search? Now imagine we have hundreds, thousands, or even millions of such influences, given to us throughout our lives. With so many gifts of knowledge from our past, assembled into this amazingly diverse world we live in, what is *our* motivation?

If we were born again, how much effort would we put into chasing our dreams? If we had another lifetime, a second chance, how much of our time would be spent watching TV, and how much time would be spent accomplishing our originally unaccomplished goals? Knowing we had lived and died before, how much urgency would there be to GET IT DONE, whatever "it" may have been?

This is the effort, the urgency and the passion we must apply to the things we believe we must do. When we allow our passion to flow, we become immortal beings. With proper diligence, we become reincarnated; all those we carry with us are reborn *in* us. Our ancestors fought and died to give human knowledge the chance to make us giants, it is our job to give it to our children. The responsibility of carrying forward the whole human race relies on those who can stand on the shoulders of giants, without becoming petty small beings; maintaining the manor of this monolith once we take in the view from the top.

Now as the representative of all the parents and grandparents and great grandparents, all the way back to the beginning. All those who gave their lives to protect a friend that later became a parent. Life after life spent surviving the elements and animals and enemies to protect the children through hundreds of thousands of years. They deserve our attention, our respect, our diligence; they are with us in our genes; they are rooting for us; they want us to succeed, to win, to accomplish, to reach, to strive, to achieve, to be happy, after all; we are all their children, lets act like it.

DEFINITIONS AND FURTHER EXPLANATIONS:

Acceptance:

One of many commonly missed hurdles on the path to maturity is the ability to *accept* reality and *handle* what *is*. When things do not go as we plan, our ability to accept and learn from them is a sign of living in the real world. Phrases like, "it is what it is," often emotionally activate those who are not yet accepting reality. Without a clear view of reality, the interfering emotional energy can have a bad influence on behavior and decision making. Other possible phrases that work in the same fashion as: "it is what it is," are: "whatever is whatever," or "however is whatever."

Attraction, The law of:

Our mind works diligently to bring us whatever we decide to focus on. If we fear pain, we shouldn't be surprised when we find it, but we will definitely find it.

Whenever we fear a thing, we give ourselves a better chance to find it. Fear is something many people obsess over. Contemplating all the verbal, visual, emotional and instinctual "keys" to our own personal fears, can and often does attract these "keys" into our lives. Anything we focus on is what our mind *thinks* we want. Fear is simply the example I use in this explanation.

The mind will notice, work on finding and bring the things we focus on, into our life and our world. The following are things we can focus on and what they can attract:

Negative:

- Thinking of the ways it is possible for people to hurt us, is often us asking: "bring me some more mean people please."

- Dwelling on what we cannot afford, is often us asking for: "more life with less money please."

- Thinking about not wanting to be alone, is often us asking: "I'd like a lonely life please."

Positive:

- Gratitude for the ways people have helped us, is often us asking for: "more generosity in my life thank you."

- Gratitude for the nice things we can afford, is often us asking for: "more prosperity in my life thank you."

- Gratitude for good friends is often us asking for: "more cool people in my life thank you."

By focusing on what we *want*, instead of what we *don't*, we give our mind a clear signal of what to look for and bring into our life.

~Try This~

Notice people holding hands, laughter in the air, smiles. Focus on finding these things or any other positive signs. Over the next few weeks or months, our perception of the world will begin to shift. We will begin to notice what we are focusing on. Maintain the process and the change will continue.

Blindness:

Blindness to our own issues makes us blind to the issues of others. This blindness allows us to choose partners who will challenge our boundary function. The amount of honesty and communication we have in our relationship, with our self, is the amount of honesty and communication we will bring to a perspective relationship. Challenges brought about by a perspective partner can help us grow, or they can drive us crazy.

The reason we don't pick the right people in our relationships when we are not clear on who we are, is because: if we don't see who *we* are, how can we see who *they* are?

Calcified Ego:

Ego that is *convinced* it has *learned all* it needs to learn, in order to *master every* issue in life. Faith and pride in our collection of knowledge that has become arrogant and boastful. The belief that we know enough, we have learned all our lessons, we can solve everyone's issues, our knowledge already has the key to every door in life, the direction for every fork in the road of life, the right words for every situation in life, etc.

Contradiction/Conflict:

Often, methods that work in one situation will not work in other situations. Many different strategies are necessary to deal with all the tests and lessons we find in life. I have found that there are several "golden rules," not just one. Many of the ideas shared in this book, come from vastly different points of view. Some of the ideas in this book will contradict each other.

See also: life according to algebra; Illusion vs. Reality

Courage: Verb

1. The act of bravery: Doing what you fear in order to get comfortable with fear.

2. Facing our fears head on/Conquering our fears with action.

Criticism:

If anyone ever says something I don't like, I laugh, because it is either a joke, or they need therapy. I look critically at their statement to see if it is founded in anything *other than them*. We can all learn to see someone else's point of view but be careful not to take the viewpoint of someone who wants to take away some of your happiness.

~Try this~

Thank people for constructive criticism. Sometimes constructive criticism can be an attempt to steal the self esteem we have created through our accomplishments. Constructive criticism is always best when it is *asked* for, not volunteered. Thanking the critic can allow us a glimpse at determining whether it is indeed constructive criticism, a joke, or merely jealousy lashing out in the form of projection. Try saying "thank you," next time someone says something un-fun, the experience is often surprising.

Ego:

Ego is faith and confidence in the abilities available, through our collection of knowledge. Ego helps drive accomplishment.

See also: Life According to Algebra.

Emotion:

1. The mammal/ emotion/ spirit; emotion is what makes certain creatures, "social creatures."

2. Emotion is the second major evolutionary change to the minds abilities. (on top of instinct)

3. The foundation of emotion and social interaction includes things like recognition, mimicry, melody and compassion.

Enlightenment: *Verb*

The act of remaining in the present moment, while effectively integrating input from the *entire* mind, to guarantee the resilience of self esteem, while accepting the world and yourself as your mother, father, brother, sister, daughter, and son, whom you love more than life itself.

The example:

In the first stages of changing behaviors, like quitting smoking, getting in shape or learning to play an instrument, there may be times when we do not feel as motivated as we did in the beginning. During these times, it is okay to take a break. This "break," is what I call "the example." We were able to make our change for a certain amount of time; we will do it again after the break, only longer. As we become comfortable in our new routine, it will become easier to maintain and we will see greater rewards from the same effort; think weightlifting.

Some of us like to remind ourselves why we decided to make a change. The best way to remember the reasons we chose to stop the old behavior, is to take a taste of the old behavior. Taste the nastiness of a cigarette, feel the sluggishness of a sedentary body, feel the energy wasted on vices instead of being spent building our dreams.

When motivation is not easy to find, try the example. Think about *why* you wanted to change while engaging in the old behavior. The path to happiness can change; it does not have to be a straight line. We can zig and zag all we want, as long as we continue forward.

Expectations:

1. Expectations are disappointments in waiting.

2. Expectations are a way to gamble our happiness on a prediction of the future.

See also: The Security Blanket Called Anger.

Explanations:

Volunteering explanations can reveal a lack of confidence in one's own abilities. If *we* know what *we* are doing, there is no need to *explain* how we did it. The only time we must explain ourselves is in a court of law. When we offer an explanation we want others to tell us we are "good boys and girls," or invade our personal boundaries, and take control and responsibility away from us.

People who have not yet learned to create their own self esteem, can get it from others in the form of approval. People raised in codependent environments often learn to gain self esteem only from outside them-selves. When one says "thank you," this is approval. When someone who has already been thanked, goes on to explain their methods without being asked, they are *seeking* more approval, and therefore more *self esteem*.

We own our explanations. We have exclusive rights to share or not to share. The ruling by the Supreme Court on Miranda v Arizona, in 1966, requires the police to remind people they have the right to remain silent. So, when Aunt Ethel asks us disapprovingly, "What were you thinking when you bought this brand of marmalade?" we can tell her, "I was thinking you can stay at someone else's house next time you come visiting."

Faith:

Faith is the ability to believe in something when there is no proof. The belief that the sun will rise is based on faith. With all the meteorites, asteroids and unpredictability in the universe, it is possible a heavenly catastrophe could wipe all life from this planet while we sleep. Faith in a future worth living is what keeps us on the path.

Fear:

Fear is a lack of knowledge and experience. To be free of fear is to *understand* the thing we fear well enough to navigate *around* it or *through* it. There is *always* something unknown, therefore there will *always* be fear; one must become comfortable feeling and experiencing fear.

Happiness Game:

Find things that make us feel good and ***schedule them into our life***.

- An exercise we enjoy: it could be feeding the birds, as long as it gets us to move a bit more than usual

- Connect with a human: shake someone's hand, send a note to a friend or relative, share a greeting with a stranger and maybe even talk about the weather

- Accept a small challenge: I bet I can fold all these cloths, wash this car, eat that hotdog, snap my fingers 50 times, etc.

Illusion & Reality

Maintaining our Illusions is important for maintaining confidence and well being. Those of us, who are most *happy* and most *successful*, often have the *least* realistic view of reality. Those with the *most* realistic view of reality are often the most *depressed* or *unhappy*.

We need both sides of a coin to be able to use it. I propose that reality and illusion are like a coin, in that one side cannot exist without the other. In order to make good decisions, we must know exactly what we are working with; so a firm grip on reality is absolutely important. However, In order to be happy and feel motivated to live our lives, we must *believe* our dreams have a "real" chance of coming true.

Paying too much attention to politics, or the troubles of the world, is not the best way to be happy. On the flip side, believing everyone on the earth is living a perfect life of luxury is no way to help spread equal rights, fair labor practices, or improve global quality of life. Both sides have their benefits and shortcomings, but when used together to help moderate each other, a sort of balance can be achieved.

Instant Gratification:

Pressure from our subconscious to live in the moment, manifests itself as Instant gratification. The need to stay in the moment can also be appeased by vices that make us at least, *partially* present. Eating, sex, thrill seeking, exercising and other similar activities, bring us *into* our bodies, *into* the moment, *into* the present. Many vices of instant gratification are completely normal behaviors, taken to an obsessive level. The pressure to appease our instant gratification becomes less insistent the more we are *in* the moment. Living in the moment requires a good relationship with our internal processes.

See also: Raising Ourselves

Instinct:

1. The reptile/ instinct/ body: the most basic part of our brain.

2. The Reptile monitors automatic bodily functions such as: the heart, lungs, stomach, bowels, reflexes etc.

3. The instinctual foundation of the mind is concerned with: grooming, mating, food, and territory. These concerns are quite

often the source of anger, fear, jealousy and aggression, to name a few.

Lessons:

- When we make "mistakes," have "issues," or have our "buttons pushed," the emotions we *feel* are *telling* us we have a lesson to learn from this moment.

- Situations that do not turn out as expected, are *full* of lessons.

- Lessons are proof that we have the *opportunity* to learn new things for the rest of our lives.

Lesson repetition:

When something happens once it is an experience, twice and it may be a coincidence, but if it happens more than three times, *we* may be the reason. Perhaps this *thing* is happening over and over just for *us*, to help *us* with a lesson.

Every emotionally charged situation is a lesson waiting to be learned. (see: Emotion As The Alarm) Until we learn the lesson, we will continue to be activated by similar situations. The activating situations will continue to happen because we have not yet *learned* how to handle that *particular* situation. The more we are activated without learning our lesson, (change the world, or change our self) the more emotional pressure we are storing in ourselves. See also: The Security Blanket Called Anger

Mistakes:

What some refer to as "Big mistakes," must be redefined as "lessons." When we define something as a "mistake," or "failure," we are punishing ourselves with a negative, self destructive perspective on the situation. The reality is, this so called "mistake," is only here to let us know we have a *lesson* to learn about our method, routine, plan, venue or course of action. There are *no* mistakes, only lessons.

"My:"

The words "my" or "mine," are the Ego stating its intent to claim rights to the self esteem attached to whatever follows these words. "This is *my* plan, *my* chicken and *my* ball." "The ball is *mine*, the chicken is *mine* and the plan is *mine*." All emotional rewards or losses are reserved with the words "my" and "mine."

Observing Ego:

- The ability to take note of our thoughts and other internal processes, as an impartial observer

- To Judge our patterns of behavior and dialogue, as if they were coming from someone else

The ability to observe ourselves objectively, allows a more honest view of ourselves. When interacting with others and ourselves, observing ego offers us a *larger* perspective of our *own* issues.

Pain:

The part of our brain responsible for reporting sensation can only process a certain amount of data at a time; it can be *overloaded*. We are most aware of our pain when we are focused on it. Sending non-pain signals will interfere with some of the pain signals, causing them to get lost in the shuffle. Simply by increasing stimulation that feels neutral to good, we can *ease* our pain.

Here are some examples of how to interfere with the pain signals: rubbing our thighs with our hands, rubbing our hands together, putting our feet in a tub of warm water, adding Alka-Seltzer to the water, using a foot massager, using a massage pad, playing an instrument, etc. Anything that does not cause pain, can be used to interfere with it. Sensations that feel good will bring more relief than we are used to experiencing, when used in conjunction with normal coping methods.

Perfection:

Perfection must have a time limit. Those of us, who are perfectionists, have an issue with setting a project down before it is "perfect."

There is an old story of a wood carver who wanted to make a little bird for his daughter. He spent several days watching birds and taking notes and drawing images of birds, until he felt he could make the *perfect* wooden toy for his daughter. He spent as much time and care picking out the *perfect* piece of wood, as he did studying birds.

As he began to carve the bird, all was going wonderfully. As he came closer to finishing the project he slowed his pace. He kept imagining all the birds he had seen, so he could make the *perfect*, final cuts to finish his daughter's gift. The little wooden bird was so *close to perfect* but each time he would turn the bird, he would see a bit of wood that did not look *perfect* and needed to be removed. With each small sliver removed, the carver planned to make the little wooden bird one cut closer to a *perfect* match for his mental image. He had worked so diligently into the night that he lost track of time and as his final candle burnt out, he nodded off.

When the wood carver awoke the next day, his body was sore from his long hours of working so delicately and so carefully. When he looked down at the table, all he saw were splinters and lumps of wood. He looked around the floor desperately for the little bird but could not find it. Then he noticed, among the splinters on the table, that there was one lump of wood that was smoother than the rest.

The old wood carver had planned to make a Quail, a Jay or a Robin but what he lifted out of the splinters, looked more like a Crane. He had carved and whittled so long and so diligently, that he had made a slim, almost sickly bird indeed. The tiny sliver of a bird was so small and so fragile, that as he turned it in his hands, it broke into several pieces.

So, the carver picked up a piece of wood at random and quickly carved a roughly shaped bird. He then sanded the bird mostly smooth and just then, his daughter burst into the shop; "You worked all night on my present again daddy, when will it be finished?" He looked at the newly carved bird which showed some signs of *imperfection,* but was still obviously the work of a master carver. His daughter followed his gaze and squealed with delight, "Oh daddy, *its perfect!*"

When we are creating, we work on a project for a time. If perfection is going to come, it will come sooner rather than later. We must put a *time limit on* attaining *perfection.* The constant striving will often drive us past our goal.

Note: time away, thinking of other things, can stimulate new directions in old ideas. When approaching perfection, take a break and give our self a chance to look on our project with new eyes. When we come back and take a new look, we may be surprised to see that we *are done*. We must be able to decide when we are close enough to perfection.

Planning:

Thought, logic and reason are the rulers of planning. Planning is the key to the future. Think of a thing you want to have happen: your 15 year high school reunion, skydiving with all of the cousins in an extended family, climbing Mt. Everest. All of the previously mentioned examples are impossible without planning. If properly planned, most things are bound to happen. Like perfection, planning has its limitations. Learn *when* to *stop* planning.

Power Phrase:

A power phrase is used to evoke understanding of a principal, course of action or inaction. Here are some examples of power phrases and what they represent:

- "Bring it" = I accept that challenge.

- "I'll get to that in a minute" = is a power phrase for procrastination.

- "Here's the deal" = is a power phrase used to state our terms.

- "So what can I do right now?" = This is a power phrase I use when I am thinking too much about what I *did*, what I *should have* done, or what I *will do*, or *should do* next time. This is a helpful phrase to remind myself, I do not live in the future or the past. Anxiety about the future or the past is **masochism**. Be nice to yourself.

Procrastination Principal:

Procrastination is usually used to describe putting off work on important tasks. Some, like me, are "Master Class Procrastinators." We can procrastinate anything, no matter how *important* or *trivial* it may be. Most people, who are aware of their procrastination, have a particular phrase, a "power Phrase." They use this power phrase to *initiate* procrastination. For example, my procrastination power phrase is: "I'll get to that in a minute."

Once you find your power phrase, you can use the phrase to turn the tables on your procrastination. I discovered I could use my power phrase to put off temptation. I was faced with vices, behaviors and options that were not in my best interests. However, I desired them none the less. I used my power phrase to put them off for a bit.

"I'll have a drink after I finish reading this page." I would then allow myself to become *immersed* in my book. I would find myself an hour later *still* reading. I would start to wonder, "Wasn't I going to have a drink?" I would then reply with, "Sure I'll have that drink in a minute."

When I am faced with a temptation, like excessive chocolate, I will simply tell myself, "I'll have that chocolate in a minute." I will then allow myself to be distracted by useful tasks, similar to the way I do when procrastinating. Use this tool on cigarettes, snacks and any other negative (vice like) thing you want to, or *should* avoid doing. The procrastination principal is like psychological judo; allowing us to use the power of procrastination to *refocus* our attention on tasks that bring us closer to achieving our dreams.

Reaction:

1. Reaction is action taken *again*.

2. Reaction is action taken *without* thought or consideration.

Consider the question: Do we like how things have turned out in our previous experience with this particular reaction? Allowing ourselves to simply re-act, *instead* of deciding on a new course of action, will *bring* us more of the same experiences.

Recapitulation:

Recapitulation is the act of recovering and releasing emotional energy invested in past events and experiences. See: Re Beginning

Resentment:

Many behaviors we are taught as children build up resentments within us. When we are asked for our "help," without the offer of some sort of compensation, we are taking advantage of ourselves for the *other* person. Regardless of what the task is, there should *always* be a pay off. Letting another person's *poor behavior* "slide," or *allowing* ourselves to be mistreated, *builds* resentment.

We can also *grow* resentment, when we don't give the gift of no. Here is an example of a person not giving the gift of "no."

His thought: "I know she wants me to buy her something nice, but I really can't afford it." His words: "Sure sweetheart, you can have whatever you want." Her thought: "I know he likes skydiving but I get motion sickness." Her words: "Skydiving sounds like a great idea."

Without the gift of "no," we have misrepresented ourselves and made the relationship more valuable than our own needs. Since a relationship is made of agreements to satisfy "mutual" needs, what good is a relationship where some needs are met with lies?

Any time we are not honest with those around us, or with ourselves, we build resentment. Resentment is anger, waiting for a reason to *explode* on someone. With enough resentment, we are *ready* to become angry about the smallest offence. Resentment is one of the most common causes of dumb arguments and the reason we sometimes argue over the most foolish things.

Selfishness:

Everything we do in life is a selfish act; we do it for its result, regardless of what *it* is. Here are some selfish reasons to do nice things:

- Taking care of grandma: because she gives affection, thanks and sometimes money.
- Volunteering for local park cleanup: to meet other likeminded people, or to feel connected to your town, or to see what changes you can make in the community.

Giving away our time and self esteem to others, in poorly negotiated interactions, drains us of our energy. If our self esteem is drained to 50%, it will take us twice as much effort to accomplish the same tasks. In the event of an emergency, the airlines instruct us to put the oxygen mask on ourselves first. We put the mask on ourselves first, so *we* will be taken care of and are then capable of helping others. Putting the mask on our selves first is a selfish act. The right amount of selfishness keeps us at our best. (Self esteem =100%) With our self esteem at 100% we can offer our best to the tasks we choose in life.

The word "selfish" has gotten a bad rap. Once we reach enlightened self interest, we look for situations that give us what *we* value, and also give the person we are interacting with something *they* value.

Shadow:

Carl Jung wrote several bits about "the shadow," simply stating: It (the shadow) may be (in part) one's link to more primitive animal instincts (Jung, C.G. 1952). Jung also wrote "Everyone carries a shadow, and the less it is embodied in the individual's conscious life, the blacker and denser it is." (Jung, C.G. (1938).

With all the socially acceptable repression going on around the world, it is easy to understand how so many of us are unaware of our shadow. It is past time we open up the lines of communication, and start the process of *integrating* our shadow into our conscious lives. (See Reflection)

Compared to a whole human mind the reptile is a relatively simple animal. The reptile is responsible for a few basic needs, they are: territory, mating, food, & grooming. As long as we have a place, mating opportunities, food to call our own and we are interested in taking care of ourselves (grooming) the reptile is satisfied.

The interruption of any of these four basic needs is felt as anger and often motivates us to fight. People fight in different ways. Fighting does not always involve a club and somebody's head. Modern fighting often involves attitude, lying, and back stabbing, among other non-deadly, methods of stealing happiness.

The mammal adds refinement to the reptile's simple list of requirements. Things like:

- curiosity to inspire exploration
- an entire library of facial expressions, voice tones, and emotions to refine our social communication
- a need to interact and make friends

The reptile sees others of its kind as either mating opportunities or competition. Adding people to our group confuses things for the reptile; who is used to the simple life of taking opportunities and beating the competition senseless. Whenever someone in our group takes away some of our basic needs the reptile wants blood. In order to work together we need to be able to trust everyone in the group not to brain us with a club. The shadow does not care about the group; the shadow cares about its place in the group, and that its own interests are top priority.

When we have destructive thoughts, we must *understand* these thoughts are simply primitive communication from the shadow. These thoughts are the shadow telling us how we feel, and what an animal would *do* about our situation. With a little imagination, we can easily figure out *why* a social animal in the wild would do some of the atrocious things that can and do pop into our heads. The dark thoughts we have about the neighbor, the bully in school, even our best friend, or family members, are NATURALY OCCURING. We *are* sane, we are just frustrated in some way, and the shadow wants to lash out.

(See Raising Ourselves)

Silent knowledge:

Ask our self any question, make the question as clear as possible and then let go of the question. Find something to do that is not related to the question and surrender to the moment. In a few hours to a few days, our subconscious will deliver our best answer, based on our current knowledge of the question.

Learning to throw a ball, swim, kiss, eat etc. does not require thought; it requires faith in the animal to improve our physical abilities. Non thinking skills are a large part of silent knowledge; a gift of the subconscious.

The plan comes from random, aimless thought. This is where the subconscious works on the problem, with all the ability of our experience. We must ask the question clearly and then remember to let it go, *be* in the moment, here, now.

We have all been witness to a group decision that was won by a voice other than the most reasonable. One person, who wants to be in charge, or right, or some other motivation besides the *good* of the *group,* can sometimes keep the best idea from rising to the top. "Ego" can be a jealous tool, which wishes to be our *only* tool. The drama that unfolds in boardrooms all over the world is happening inside our heads. Ego can push any plan down if we are not paying attention. See also: Life According To Algebra.

When our thoughts are still and we are relaxed in the present moment, ideas and inspiration can come rising to the surface.

Strength:

Strength starts with a willingness to "step up," in the moment. In order to stand we must have self esteem to power our confidence. A belief in our abilities comes from defending our rights, and the rights of others. Even if we have a group of personal assistants, they cannot look after our every need as well as we can. We are helpless without the kind of protection only *we* can offer *ourselves*. We must be willing to be strong for ourselves if we want to be strong for others, and vice versa.

Recognizing when *others* see us as a role model makes us more capable of *being* the person we want to be. Accepting the ability to lead by example strengthens our confidence and fills our self esteem.

Stress

Stress is a lack of congruence with ourselves, between our beliefs/thoughts/mind, feelings/emotions/spirit, and needs/instincts/body.

Stress is a bad practical joke we play on ourselves, again and again. Stress can make any issue we are having, worse.

Subconscious:

1. Instinct and emotion.

2. The mind that is not logic, spoken language, or reason.

3. That which is aware but not *conscious* as is thought.

4. The source of "silent knowledge."

Switch, The:

When we learn new boundary function, it is often necessary to speak and act differently with people who are used to dealing with the "old us." Standing up to and confronting people we are not used to asserting our rights with, requires a switch in our programmed behavior.

Pick someone with whom it is easy to honestly enforce our boundaries. The person you use as your "switch" could be a sibling, a customer, a coworker, our dog, the mailman or even an imaginary friend. Use them as inspiration when confronted with someone who is *not* so easy to work with. The next time you are dealing with a difficult person, imagine you are talking to your "switch." Ask: "what would I say if this were my customer, coworker, etc. (or whomever is easiest to honestly enforce our boundaries with)?"

Thought:

1. The primate/ thought/ logic/ reason.

2. The newest processes of the brain (on top of emotion, on top of instinct)

3. The foundation of reason, spoken language, time sense, etc.

I wrote this book because I couldn't remember it all at once.

The methods inside have helped me stay on my path,

I hope they make *your* path a bit easier to follow.

CREDITS AND NOTES:

Triune Brain Theory: Caine, Renate Nummela and Geoffrey Caine. (1990). *Making Connections: Teaching and the Human Brain.* Nashville, TN: Incentive Publications.

Notes: The triune brain theory was disproved almost as soon as it was published. The metaphor of the three parts of the mind matches up so elegantly to so many other theories, theologies, philosophies and so on, I decided to use it to break down, and begin to simplify the structure of my psyche. Who knew I would get to share it with so many.

Recapitulation: Castaneda, Carlos. (1982). *The Eagles Gif.* New York, NY: Simon & Schuster.

Petty tyrant: Castaneda, Carlos (1984) *The Fire From Within*. New York, NY: Simon & Schuster.

EMDR: (Eye Movement Desensitization and Reprocessing) Shapiro, F. (1989). *Journal of Traumatic Stress, 2*, 199-223.

Boundary function: Dobransky, Paul. M.D. (2005) *"Mind O.S."*

Notes: seminar style presentation available online. (Amazing stuff)

Self Hypnosis: Milton H. Erickson M.D. I could not find the source of the quote from Dr. Erickson. It may not have been in his printed works. Milton Erickson is one of the millions of people I want to thank for their contribution to the knowledge base of the human race. Milton H. Erickson is arguably the father of modern hypnosis, and his life story is an inspiration all by itself. Born: December 5, 1901, Nevada Died: March 25, 1980, Phoenix, AZ. Education: University of Wisconsin-Madison.

Memes: Brodie, Richard. (1996). *Virus of the Mind*. Seattle Wa: Integral press. (good read)

Observing Ego/awareness: Krishnamurti, J. (1972). *The flight of the Eagle*. New York NY: Harper & Row.   Notes: Changed my perception. (Good Read)

Quote: Millman, D. (Writer), Bernhardt, K. (Writer), & Salva, V. (Director) (2006). *Peaceful warrior* [DVD]. (Lessons in Distraction and Awareness)

Dexter Raising ourselves/shadow: Manos Jr., J. (Writer), Lindsay, J. (Writer), Rosenberg, M. (Writer), & Goldwyn, T. (Director) (2007). An inconvenient lie [Television series season 2 episode 3]. In Cerone, D. (Executive Producer), *Dexter*. Showtime.

Quote: McCulloch, C. (Director), McCulloch, C. (Writer), & Hammer, D. (Writer) (2013). What color is your cleansuit? [Television series episode]. In McCulloc, C. (Executive Producer), *The Venture Brothers*. Turner Broadcasting System. Retrieved from www.cartoonnetwork.com

Quote: Kowalczyk, E. (1994) "I Alone" [Recorded by Ed Kowalczyk, Patrick Dahlheimer, Chad Gracey & Chad Taylor] On *Throwing Copper* [CD]. Fort Lauderdale, Florida: Radioactive records.

Projection: Freud,S.(1979). *Case Histories II.* PELICAN BOOKS *(PFL 9) p. 132*

"link to ones…" Jung, C.G. (1952). "Answer to Job." In CW 11: Psychology and Religion: West and East. P.12

"Everyone carries…" Jung, C.G. (1938). "Psychology and Religion." In CW 11: Psychology and Religion: West and East. P.131

Additional reading:

The power of honesty: Blanton, Brad. (2000). *Radical Honesty.* Stanley VA: Sparrowhawk Publishing. (Good Read)

Tough Love: Farrelly, Frank & Brandsma, Jeff. (1974) *Provocative therapy.* Cupertino Ca: Meta Publications. (Good Read)

Acceptance: Batchelor, Stephen. (1997). *Buddhism without Beliefs.* New York NY: Berkley Publishing group. (Good Read)

About the Author:

Jesse grew up in Monterey County and has always had a love for creative problem solving. Jesse found people and his own mind to be the best source for interesting puzzles. Jesse achieved his Associates degree in Psychology from the University of Phoenix. Jesse is also a musician and a functional artist, creating pieces whose beauty is in both form and function. He currently resides in Carmel, California with his wife Keeza who is also an artist.

Made in the USA
San Bernardino, CA
13 January 2014